ARCHITECTURE

BLYTHE CAMENSON

SECOND EDITION

New York Chicago San Francisco Lisbon London Madrid Mexico City
Milan New Delhi San Juan Seoul Singapore Sydney Toronto

The McGraw·Hill Companies

Library of Congress Cataloging-in-Publication Data

Camenson, Blythe.
Careers in architecture / by Blythe Camenson.—2nd ed.
p. cm.
Includes bibliographical references.
ISBN 13: 978-0-07-154556-3 (alk. paper)
ISBN 10: 0-07-154556-5 (alk. paper)
1. Architecture—Vocational guidance—United States. I. Title.

NA1995.C257 2008
720.23—dc22 2008024657

1 2 3 4 5 6 7 8 9 10 11 12 13 14 15 16 17 18 19 20 21 DOC/DOC 0 9 8

ISBN 978-0-07-154556-3
MHID 0-07-154556-5

This book is printed on acid-free paper.

CONTENTS

ACKNOWLEDGMENTS

The author would like to thank the following professionals for providing information about their careers:

Joel André, architect
Peter Benton, architect
Greg Blackwell, landscape architect/interiorscaper
Kent Brinkley, landscape architect/garden historian
David DiCicco, architect
John Downs, professor
Gary Fischer, architect
George Hallowell, architect
Julie Haney, architect
Jasper (Joe) Hardesty, architect
Steve Lazarian, licensed general contractor
Judy Moore, architect
Harvey Schorr, architect
Lee Sullivan Hill, cost estimator
Maggie Shannon Wagenaar, civil engineer
Matthew I. Zehnder, landscape architect/regional planner

PART ONE

Careers in Architecture

THE FIELD OF ARCHITECTURE

Architecture is the profession of designing buildings, open areas, and even whole communities, often with an eye to the aesthetics of the end result. The word architecture also refers to the overall design: the architecture of New Orleans, of Paris, and so on.

Architects are the trained professionals who design buildings and other structures. The design of a building involves far more than its appearance, however. Buildings must be functional, safe, and economical, and they must suit the needs of the people who use them. The architect who designs a new library and forgets to calculate the weight of the books the floor needs to support is doing his or her client and the community a disservice and will not be in business for long. Architects must take every detail into consideration when they design buildings and other structures.

A HISTORY OF ARCHITECTURAL EDUCATION

Massachusetts Institute of Technology (MIT) in Cambridge, Massachusetts, was the first institution to offer formal education in architecture. The year was 1865, some fifty years after Thomas Jefferson, the United States' only architect-president, proposed a professional curriculum in architecture be established in the School of Mathematics of the University of Virginia. Because the search for an appropriately trained instructor yielded no one, the program was delayed for many years.

In 1867, the University of Illinois at Urbana and, in 1871, Cornell University followed MIT. Canada entered the field of training architects with the Universities of Toronto and Montreal in 1876.

The Morrill Act, which the U.S. Congress passed in 1862, affected the focus of higher education for architecture, as well as other fields. In exchange for land granted by the U.S. government (thus, the term land-grant colleges), colleges were directed to provide practical, hands-on education for U.S. students. This approach contrasted with the European style that more clearly separated education and training. In other words, you were "educated" at the university and, once on the job, you were "trained." Although not all institutions of higher education founded since then are land-grant colleges, the tradition of the system developed was pervasive, particularly in the South, Midwest, and West. In spite of the American land-grant influence, however, the European tradition also had an important historical impact in architectural education in North America.

Many people thought the practical education approach to be uncultured. Looking to Europe for guidance, as Americans often did in the nineteenth century, attention focused on the distinguished École des Beaux-Arts in Paris as the epitome of architectural training. The Beaux Arts philosophy was imported to the United States, and most architecture schools at the beginning of the twentieth century had at least one Paris-trained professor. Those who were not lucky enough to have a French architect as an instructor could travel to Paris and attend the program there for a year. Graduate courses in New York were taught by members of the Beaux Arts staff. Canada imported a number of Beaux Arts–trained teachers at this time, but because Canada had a stronger connection with England than did the United States, many of Canada's first instructors came from the British Isles.

The jury system still in place today to judge art shows and other artistic events developed as a result of the Beaux Arts system. Students were assigned a design problem early in the first term, and their progress in solving this problem was watched and encouraged through close supervision. By the end of the period, drawings were delivered to the "master" for critique. The Beaux Arts system relied heavily on brilliant teachers and on learning by doing. Competition was intense, and the end results were beautifully drawn projects in traditional styles that were often workable only on the basis of "good taste" and intuition. The style was mostly neoclassical, and the favorite building type was the monument. These creative projects were judged by a jury of highly regarded professors and guest architects.

In the early part of the twentieth century, the United States and Canada developed their own cultures and shied away from European influence. Changes in architecture in Europe, the growing fame of Chicago skyscrapers, and Frank Lloyd Wright's "Prairie School" architecture contributed to change in North America.

Architectural education started in at least five ways on different campuses: separate and autonomous schools or colleges of architecture; departments and programs within graduate schools; schools of art or design; schools oriented toward engineering, technology, or sociology; and, more recently, schools of urban planning and design. For example, the University of Oregon's architecture program, started in 1914, was the first in the United States to affiliate itself with the allied arts—painting, crafts, and sculpture—rather than with engineering. Columbia University shifted in 1934 away from the Beaux Arts method toward those of the modern German movement highlighted by the Bauhaus school. The Bauhaus, formed in 1919, moved to its famous Dessau, Germany, location in 1925 but was closed down by the Nazis in 1933. The influence of that school was felt throughout the world. Instruction was of a practical nature, providing actual work for buildings under construction.

In 1936, Walter Gropius, the director of the Bauhaus, came to the United States and headed the architecture department at Harvard University from 1938 to 1952. In the same year, Harvard joined architecture, landscape architecture, and urban planning into one school, the triangular model for many schools today. Two years later, the famous architect Ludwig Mies van der Rohe—a colleague of Gropius—came to the United States and become the head of the architecture school at the Illinois Institute of Technology. In 1922, Cornell University was the first school to adopt a five-year professional program of study in architecture. By 1940, this became standard practice in all architecture schools.

Architecture continues to change and increase in complexity. Projects in general are larger, with many new technological developments, such as factory prefabrication or automatic control systems for air conditioning. Efficient use of energy and ecologically responsible design has become important.

Another change is today's client. Architects work with more than private individuals. Often, today's client is a board of directors or trustees, a special committee, or representatives of a government agency.

THE DUTIES OF THE ARCHITECT

Though architects generally start their careers from the same starting place—a professional degree in architecture—the paths they take from that point onward will vary. Architects can play many roles, with many settings to play them in. Architecture is not a profession that will stifle its members.

Architects provide professional services to individuals and organizations planning a construction project. They may be involved in all phases of development, from the initial discussion with the client through the entire construction process. The architect and client discuss the objectives, requirements, and budget of a project. In some cases, architects provide various predesign services: conducting feasibility and environmental impact studies, selecting a site, or specifying the requirements the design must meet. For example, they may determine space requirements by researching the number and type of potential users of a building. Architects then prepare drawings and a report presenting ideas for the client to review.

After the initial proposals are discussed and accepted, architects develop final construction plans. These plans show the building's appearance and details for its construction, accompanied by drawings of the structural system; air-conditioning, heating, and ventilating systems; electrical systems; plumbing; and possibly site and landscape plans. Architects specify the building materials and, in some cases, the interior furnishings. In developing designs, architects follow building codes, zoning laws, fire regulations, and other ordinances, such as those requiring easy access by disabled persons.

Throughout the planning stage, they make necessary changes. Although they have traditionally used pencil and paper to produce design and construction drawings, architects are increasingly turning to computer-aided design and drafting (CADD) technology for these important tasks.

Architects may assist the client in obtaining construction bids, selecting a contractor, and negotiating the construction contract. As construction proceeds, they may visit the building site to ensure the contractor is following the design, adhering to the schedule, using the specified materials, and meeting quality work standards.

The job is not complete until all construction is finished, required tests are made, and construction costs are paid. Sometimes, architects provide postconstruction services, such as facilities management. They advise on energy efficiency measures, evaluate how well the building design adapts to the needs of occupants, and make necessary improvements.

WORKING CONDITIONS FOR ARCHITECTS

Architects usually work in a comfortable environment. Most of the time, they are in their offices consulting with clients, developing reports and drawings, and working with other architects and engineers. They often visit construction sites to review the progress of projects. Architects may occasionally be under stress, working nights and weekends to meet deadlines. Almost two out of five architects work more than forty hours a week, in contrast to one in four workers in all other occupations combined.

EMPLOYMENT OPPORTUNITIES

Because of the unusual scope of architecture programs, public and private sectors offer opportunities for architecture degree holders. In addition to traditional practice in private architectural firms, architecture graduates are commonly employed in public and government agencies, community design and urban planning firms, building and construction firms, community development corporations, and building products manufacturers. Alternate career paths may lead into related disciplines discussed later in this chapter.

JOB OUTLOOK FOR ARCHITECTS

Prospective architects may face competition for entry-level jobs, especially if the number of architectural degrees awarded remains at current levels or increases. Employment of architects is projected to grow faster than the average for all occupations through 2016, and additional job openings will stem from the need to replace architects who retire or leave the labor force for other reasons. Many individuals are attracted to this occupation, and the number of applicants often exceeds the number of available jobs, especially in the most prestigious firms. Prospective architects who complete at least one summer internship—paid or unpaid—while in school and who know CADD technology (especially CADD technology that conforms to the new National CAD Standard) will have a distinct advantage in obtaining an intern-architect position after graduation.

Employment of architects is tied to the level of local construction, particularly nonresidential structures such as office buildings, shopping centers, schools, and health-care facilities. After a boom in nonresidential construction during the 1980s, building slowed significantly during the first half of the 1990s. Despite slower labor force growth and increases in telecommuting and flexiplace work, however, nonresidential construction is expected to grow more quickly through 2008 than during the previous decade, driving demand for more architects.

As buildings age, demand for remodeling and repair work should grow considerably. The needed renovation and rehabilitation of old buildings, particularly in urban areas where space for new buildings is becoming limited, is expected to provide many job opportunities for architects.

Demographic trends and changes in health-care delivery are influencing the demand for certain institutional structures and should provide more jobs for architects. Growth is expected in the number of adult care centers, assisted-living facilities, and community health clinics, all being preferable, less costly alternatives to hospitals and nursing homes. Growth in Sunbelt states' population will continue to add demand for residential and work space. In addition, increases in the school-age population have resulted in new school construction. Additions to existing schools (especially colleges and universities), as well as overall modernization, will continue to add to the demand for architects through 2016.

Because construction—particularly office and retail construction—is sensitive to cyclical changes in the economy, architects will face particularly strong competition for jobs or clients during recessions, and layoffs may occur. Those involved in the design of institutional buildings such as schools, hospitals, nursing homes, and correctional facilities will be less affected by fluctuations in the economy.

Even in times of overall good job opportunities, the country will have areas with poor opportunities. Architects who are licensed to practice in one state must meet the licensing requirements of other states before practicing elsewhere, but these requirements are becoming more standardized, facilitating movement between states.

TYPES OF ARCHITECTURAL OFFICES

Architectural practices are usually structured on one of two basic models. The first consists of a series of departmental specializations: designers, specification writers, structural experts, landscape designers, and production draftspeople. A project starts in one division and is passed to the next as work progresses. In such instances, few people will see the job all the way through to completion, but each will perform a specific function for each job the office undertakes.

The other model divides the office into teams, with each team responsible for its own projects from start to finish. Various specialists may be on the team, with consultants involved. A team may be working on several jobs simultaneously but will have little, if any, responsibility for other projects being undertaken by other teams.

Few offices precisely fit these simplified models, and many have certain aspects of both. Some architectural firms subcontract with consultants and other firms for major portions of the project, thus keeping their own staff to a minimal number. In fact, principals of large firms may spend little of their time on actual design or drawings for new buildings. Architects working in large firms are not solely responsible for a complete building. A large and complex building, such as a hospital costing $100 million, may require three to four years from preliminary programming to completion, with as many as forty people working nearly full-time on this one project.

Depending on the particular model a firm follows, the roles for architects may range from design to management or anywhere in between. Though larger firms may offer opportunities to specialize in a particular aspect of the practice, smaller firms often require the architect to master many different facets of the profession. Common practice roles include project management, facilities planning, site planning and design, technical research and specifications, document production, contract administration, urban design and planning, interior design, and practice management.

GETTING THAT FIRST JOB

New graduates usually begin as intern-architects in architectural firms, where they assist in preparing architectural documents or drawings. They may do research on building codes and materials, or write specifications for building materials, installation criteria, the quality of finishes, and other related details. Internship for those graduates working toward an ultimate goal of licensure to practice architecture is intended as a continuation of the process of architectural education, providing specialized training and knowledge about architectural practice not usually covered in the academic setting.

New graduates often seek a private architecture firm as the setting for their first job. For interns, diversified experience under the supervision of a registered architect in such a firm is the fastest and most typical way to fulfill the training requirements for registration. But, because most firms are small, interns rarely see the first place of employment as the ultimate one. Rather, this is a chance to learn and contribute, develop the everyday practice skills, and better understand where each intern's place may be within the profession and the building enterprise.

An internship is a two-way street though. The employer expects the intern to bring basic professional skills to the job, to use those skills in performing professional services, and to learn how the firm practices architecture. As in any employment setting, the goals of the intern and firm may not overlap completely. The secret to a successful internship lies in exploiting and expanding the area of overlap as quickly and as effectively as possible.

Some firms take a strong interest in the growth of their interns, pointing toward registration as an architect and expanded responsibilities leading to those of the project architect. These firms may be active in the Intern Development Program (IDP) and, if so, will provide specific opportunities for the growth and development of their interns (see Chapter 2). For most firms, however, the process is less structured. To meet the demands of projects and clients within tight economic constraints, a firm does not have much time or money for intern development.

For interns, professional development is important. When choosing the first position, the American Institute of Architects (AIA) suggests you use this list of questions as a guide:

- What is the firm's basic attitude toward me as an intern? Am I there to "fill a slot," or is the firm interested in my professional growth?
- What are my long-term prospects for remaining with the firm? Will I move on after I am licensed, or will I remain?
- Does the firm invest in my professional growth?
- Will I have opportunities to participate in education programs? Will I have time to prepare for the registration exam?
- Will I have a mentor?
- Does the firm participate in the Intern Development Program?

The answers to these questions do not all have to be yes. Interns consider many factors in selecting a firm. If they are on the path to registration, though, personal growth and diversity of experience are important. For further investigation, look at the firms in the region(s) you are considering. CMD Group's ProFile (www.cmdg) is a good place to start as it provides contacts, telephone numbers, and enough information about a practice to help you select some firms. Your local AIA chapter office may publish classified listings or maintain a file of job opportunities in your area. Check the AIA website for current job listings (aiaonline.com).

Many other valuable sources of information exist for job opportunities in this field, including your local architecture school. Many employers post job listings in college and university architecture departments, even for experienced people. Some schools maintain placement services for students and alumni. You should never underestimate the power of word-of-mouth and networking, so keep in touch with classmates. Most schools maintain current addresses of alumni, and you may want to scan these for contacts in firms or other practice settings that interest you. Finally, look around at what is being proposed and built. Who is doing work that interests you? These would be people to contact.

STARTING YOUR OWN FIRM

Once the architect has fulfilled internship requirements and is registered, opportunities for firm ownership are a real possibility. Reasons to move into self-employment can vary: perhaps partnership in the current employer's firm doesn't seem likely, or philosophies clash or differ. As a professional of small (and often closely held) firms, the goal of ownership is most frequently achieved by starting up a firm, whether as a sole proprietor or in collaboration with one or two others with common goals and ideally with complementary skills. About a thousand new firms start up each year.

SAMPLE INTERN JOB OPENINGS

These listings are provided as a sample only, and as such, the hiring firms are not mentioned. You can locate similar listings by searching the Internet using various keywords: architecture, jobs, careers.

Intern, Georgia
An international firm located in Atlanta is seeking an intern-architect to work on commercial projects including aviation, military, industrial, sports, and criminal justice facilities. Qualified candidates will have architectural degree or background (NAAB-accredited professional degree preferred), approximately zero to three years' experience, CADD literate (Microstation preferred) with good graphic capabilities and verbal communication skills. Competitive salary and benefits package.

Intern, Mississippi
Small firm focusing in historic preservation, new construction within the context of historic buildings, and innovative residential projects seeks enthusiastic intern-architect with a desire to work and live in a great small town in Mississippi. Individual will bring fresh, creative ideas to work on award-winning projects. Bachelor's degree in architecture, AutoCAD proficiency, and a keen desire to advance your skills. Excellent working environment and comprehensive benefits.

Intern, Texas
Large Texas firm has a full-time position available for an intermediate architect or intern with two to six years' experience in commercial architecture. We prefer a candidate with strong design and production skills who is seeking a ground-level opportunity with a growing architectural practice. The position offers long-term commitment

and career advancement for the right individual. Staff members are offered the option of a traditional office workplace or working from a remote home office with flexible hours. The successful candidate will be a responsible, self-motivated, proactive individual who enjoys a degree of autonomy in the workplace. Experience with ArchiCAD is a plus.

EARNINGS FOR ARCHITECTS

Architecture, in general, is not a career that brings much fame and fortune. Only a few architects have become household names through the ages. Architectural employees may be paid an hourly wage or an annual salary. According to a 2005 AIA survey, the average compensation, including bonuses, for intern-architects in architectural firms was $38,800. Managers and department heads had average earnings of $85,500; senior architects and designers who were not managers or principals of a firm earned $57,700. These salaries are much less than for the related engineering fields (see Chapter 7). Principals or partners of firms had average earnings of $159,800, although partners in some large practices earned considerably more. Similar to other industries, small architectural firms (fewer than ten employees) are less likely than larger firms to provide employee benefits, though some firms have profit-sharing plans for those who are not partners.

Earnings of partners in established architectural firms may fluctuate because of changing business conditions. Some architects may have difficulty establishing their own practices and may go through a period when their expenses are greater than their income, requiring substantial financial resources.

RELATED FIELDS

Architects—and sometimes interns approaching registration—discover many settings exist in which to develop their skills and interests. Some seek community design and urban planning firms (see Chapter 8), public agencies, and private community development corporations. Others find the construction environment more to their taste, finding positions with contractors, developers, and building products manufacturers or suppliers (see Chapter 9). Still others discover they can manage and design projects within corporate, institutional, and governmental facilities offices.

Some career paths lead out of architecture practice and into related activities, such as architectural history, historic preservation (Chapter 4), or computer-aided design; allied disciplines, including planning, landscape architecture (Chapter 6), engineering (Chapter 7), or interior design; or related industries, such as computer software development, real estate, finance, or law. Teaching and research provide yet another practice setting for many architecture graduates (Chapter 5). Some of these alternate career paths do not require architectural licensure but may necessitate additional education, training, or certification required by the particular allied profession.

What follows is a look at some related fields. Other alternative and related fields are covered in subsequent chapters.

Interior Design

Interior design requires expertise in areas such as space planning, finish materials, acoustics, lighting, selection and purchase of furnishings and furniture, and ergonomic and behavioral sciences, that is, the nonstructural aspects of building interiors. Specialties have emerged in the interior design of commercial offices, stage sets, retail stores, hotels, restaurants, historic styles and preservation, ship and aircraft interiors, and furniture design. Many colleges and universities offer undergraduate and graduate programs in interior architecture and interior design, and some states license or certify interior designers.

Lighting Design

The lighting designer's challenge is to illuminate with purpose, providing visual comfort, efficiency, productivity, and, in some cases, drama. Successful lighting designers combine an aesthetic sense of color and form, a solid grasp of the technology of light (lamps, fixtures, controls, and accessories), and an ability to integrate natural and artificial lighting in architecture. Many of today's practicing lighting designers are trained as interior or industrial designers or as electrical engineers, though architecture schools are becoming important participants in lighting education and research.

Acoustical Design

The demand for proper acoustics is inherent in all building types. Good acoustics are as important for comfort and productivity in homes, offices, schools, and shopping centers as they are in churches and concert halls. Increasingly, acousticians must know how to work with the electronic systems that control or enhance existing sound in space or even how to "shape" space for listening. Educated as engineers, physicists, and occasionally architects, acousticians usually work as independent consultants in small firms.

Environmental and Behavioral Research

In their pursuit of foundations in research for design and building, some architects move in behavioral directions, doing advanced study in environmental design, psychology, or sociology. These individuals often seek teaching and research appointments. Some form consultancies offering postoccupancy evaluations and participating in the facilities-management process.

FIRSTHAND ACCOUNTS

What better way to learn about a field than to hear from those personally involved in it? Included throughout this book are firsthand accounts from a range of residential, commercial, historic preservation, and landscape architects, as well as engineers and planners. You will note throughout these accounts that many architects work for firms that choose not to specialize in only one area of architecture, and that these firms keep specialists on staff in various areas. This keeps firms much more competitive with others in the marketplace. Read what these professionals have to say about getting started and what the work is like, including the upsides and downsides. Then make your own conclusions.

Choosing a career in architecture can lead you in a number of different directions. The more informed you are, the more informed your choices can be, and the more ultimately satisfying your career will be.

CHAPTER 2

PREPARING FOR A CAREER IN ARCHITECTURE

As of January 1999, in the United States, to call yourself an architect you must have a license issued by a state, the District of Columbia, or a U.S. territory. Architecture school graduates may work in the field before they are licensed, but a licensed architect is required to take legal responsibility for all work. Licensing requirements include a professional degree in architecture, a period of practical training or internship, and passage of all sections of the Architect Registration Examination (ARE).

The National Architectural Accrediting Board (NAAB), established in 1940, is the sole agency authorized to accredit U.S. professional degrees in architecture. Since most state registration boards in the United States require any applicant for licensure to have graduated from an NAAB-accredited program, obtaining such a degree is an essential aspect of preparing for the professional practice of architecture. However, state architectural registration boards set their own standards, so not graduating from a non–NAAB-accredited program may meet the educational requirement for licensing in some states. There are currently 107 schools in the United States and 10 in Canada offering professional programs in architecture, leading to the Bachelor of Architecture or Master of Architecture degree (see Appendix C). The University of Hawaii at Manoa offers only a Doctor of Architecture degree.

TYPES OF DEGREES

Several types of professional degrees in architecture are available through colleges and universities. The majority of all architectural degrees are from five-year Bachelor of Architecture programs, intended for students entering from high school or with no previous architectural training. Some schools offer a two-year Master of Architecture program for students with a preprofessional undergraduate degree in architecture or a related area or offer a three- or four-year Master of Architecture program for students with a degree in another discipline. In addition, many programs will combine and vary the above options.

The choice of degree depends upon each individual's preference and educational background. Prospective architecture students should consider the available options before committing to a program. For example, even though the five-year Bachelor of Architecture program offers the fastest route to the professional degree, courses are specialized and, if the student does not complete the program, moving to a nonarchitectural program may be difficult.

All degrees outside of the field of architecture are referred to as nonarchitecture degrees. This title generally describes degrees in fields such as philosophy, biology, engineering, and undesignated bachelor of arts and bachelor of science degrees. These undesignated B.A. or B.S. degrees can provide opportunities for a major or minor in architectural studies or environmental design offered through a liberal studies program. Architecture degrees fit into one of four categories: preprofessional architecture degrees, professional architecture degrees, postprofessional architecture degrees, and nonprofessional graduate architecture degrees.

Preprofessional Architecture Degree

This term refers to architecturally focused four-year degrees that are not professional degrees and, thus, cannot be accredited. These degrees have such titles as B.S. in Architecture, B.S. in Architectural Studies, B.A. in Architecture, Bachelor of Environmental Design, Bachelor of Architectural Studies. The amount of architecture work in the program varies and will determine the length of time required to complete further professional architecture studies.

Professional Architecture Degree

A professional architecture degree is one that may be accredited by the NAAB or Canadian Architectural Certification Board (CACB). Accredited degrees are required by most jurisdictions for licensure as an architect. These degrees are a Bachelor of Architecture (B.Arch.) degree or a Master of Architecture (M.Arch.) degree. The Bachelor of Architecture normally requires at least five years to complete. The Master of Architecture requires from one to five years to complete depending on the individual student's previous education. When the master's degree follows a four-year preprofessional architecture degree, it will represent the "two" in the term four-plus-two program and will be the final portion of the professional phase of the study program.

Postprofessional Architecture Degree

This is a graduate degree offered to students who have a professional degree in architecture. Such degree programs are not accredited by NAAB and CACB. The degrees may be in highly specialized areas of study such as design theory, health-care facilities, preservation, interior design, solar design, and so on. This type of degree can be a master's degree or, in a few cases, a Ph.D. or other doctorate degree.

Nonprofessional Graduate Architecture Degree

This title refers to graduate degrees in architecture offered to students who do not have a professional degree and wish to pursue nonprofessional graduate work in architecture. These programs vary widely in duration and degree title.

PATHS TO THE PROFESSIONAL DEGREE

The following three paths exist to obtaining the professional degree in architecture. The majority of students enter architecture through the first two routes; however, the third route is viable. Detailed explanations of each of these paths are offered after the list.

1. Obtaining a Bachelor of Architecture degree
2. Obtaining a preprofessional degree plus a professional Master of Architecture degree (the four-plus-two route falls in this category)
3. Obtaining a four-year nonarchitecture degree plus a three-year to four-year professional Master of Architecture degree

Path 1: Bachelor of Architecture Degree

The professional Bachelor of Architecture degree can be the most expeditious means of obtaining the professional degree required for licensure. This route normally requires a minimum of five years of study followed by a three-year internship.

Although a five-year program provides the quickest route to satisfy the academic requirements for licensure, speed is not necessarily synonymous with what may be best for every individual. Many Bachelor of Architecture programs begin with a concentration of architecture courses in a fairly prescribed manner, though some schools begin with a general course of instruction. Electives tend to be few and exposure to other fields limited. As a result, the approximately 50 percent of entering students who do not complete the program may have difficulty moving into another area without some loss of credit.

Many Bachelor of Architecture programs, however, have devised flexible curriculum structures. These programs are broken into yearly components separating the general instruction and preprofessional requirements from the concentration of architecture courses that follows in two-plus-three, one-plus-four, three-plus-two, or four-plus-one year programs. The breaks between the program's components indicate logical entry and exit points from the various phases of the full five-year program.

In most schools, the student's work is carefully reviewed before advancement to the next phase. Such points provide an easy means of transfer into an architecture program, transfer to another institution (particularly between degrees), or transfer to another academic discipline. The logical break points may be used by the faculty to transfer students who have demonstrated little progress. The early segments of the curriculum mix preprofessional design courses with liberal arts and can serve as a common base for several different environmental design disciplines such as architecture, landscape architecture, industrial design, or graphic design.

Most professional degree programs accept transfer students at the designated break points, but transfer credit is usually evaluated on an individual course-by-course and case-by-case basis, though the structure of some programs makes it relatively easy for a professional school to accept transfer students from junior colleges and other colleges. A student considering an architecture degree should start at the professional school or at a school with a preprofessional program.

Path 2: Preprofessional Bachelor's Plus Master of Architecture Degree

The preprofessional degree plus professional Master of Architecture degree is the other predominant route to obtaining a professional architecture degree. This route normally requires six years to complete, followed by a three-year internship. The program is flexible. At the end of four years, the student has a college degree and may decide to continue in architecture and get a professional master's degree, spend a year or two working for an architect, or change disciplines and pursue study in another design-related field. The graduate may decide at this point to shift careers completely and/or seek an advanced degree outside the design field.

Preprofessional programs are not professionally accredited and vary widely with respect to title, emphasis, electives, requirements, and specific architecture offerings. They are, however, preparatory for advanced architectural or other environmental design fields. The four-year preprofessional program may be subdivided into two phases, usually of two years each. The prearchitecture program may have only basic introductory courses in architecture with the majority of the course work focusing on the arts, humanities, and sciences. The typical program, like the subdivided five-year professional programs, is highly flexible and provides a general education in the early years. Though this may frustrate many who want to immerse themselves quickly in architecture, it does provide time for experiencing a wider range of subjects, allowing the maturing student a better opportunity to make career choices. Ideally, the extra courses in the humanities and social sciences will give students a broader background from which to start their professional education. For those who ultimately receive advanced degrees in design areas other than architecture or in nonarchitecture subjects (such as business or structural engineering), the four-year degree may be preferable to the five-year professional program in minimizing course work and time. One other advantage of a four-plus-two program is the potential for earning the professional degree at an institution other than where the undergraduate work was completed.

The graduate degree component of the four-plus-two path is the professional NAAB- or CACB-accredited (for Canada) degree. This degree is appropriate for students who have a four-year preprofessional undergraduate degree in architecture. The course of study generally takes two years. However, at some schools, up to three years is required. These programs provide the professional education of the student as well as an opportunity for independent and creative exploration. The master's degree program must be accredited if the student wishes to obtain the professional degree and licensure.

In addition to the standard four-plus-two path, the NAAB has recently recognized a five-and-a-half-year Master of Architecture program, which the student may enter from high school. In this case, students enroll in a program that may lead directly to a Master of Architecture degree, following a curriculum that is similar to that of a Bachelor of Architecture program. Students must be expressly accepted into the university's graduate school to pursue the degree's final phase. Those who do not qualify for graduate study have the option of completing a nonprofessional undergraduate degree, with the possibility of pursuing the master's degree in one of the more traditional paths at another institution.

Several schools are now considering converting their B.Arch. programs to M.Arch. programs, either along the lines described above or by offering a bachelor's degree and an M.Arch. simultaneously at the end of a five-year or five-and-a-half-year period of study.

Path 3: Nonarchitecture Bachelor's Plus Master of Architecture Degree

The nonarchitecture degree plus professional master's degree path is the third route available but is the least traveled option. This route normally requires seven-and-a-half years of study (a four-year undergraduate degree plus a three-and-a-half-year Master of Architecture degree), followed by a three-year internship. This route is usually taken by those who have embarked on a career other than architecture and later decide to study architecture. Many people enter the profession this way. Their average age is in the late twenties, and their undergraduate backgrounds range across every discipline. Students entering the profession this way are usually quite mature and serious about their studies. This course of study requires three to four years beyond the undergraduate degree. The immersion into architecture is quick and intense. Some schools provide all of the education at the graduate level. Others will admit degree holders into their professional master's program with "deficiencies." This means that preparatory undergraduate course work must first be successfully completed before formal admittance to the graduate program. Like the two-year Master of Architecture degree, the three-and-a-half year M.Arch. may be a fully NAAB- or CACB-accredited professional degree program, and successful graduates have professional education credentials equal to those with a B.Arch. or other M.Arch degrees.

COURSE OF STUDY

A typical program includes courses in architectural history and theory, building design, professional practice, math, physical sciences, and liberal arts.

Central to most architectural programs is the design studio, where students practice the skills and concepts learned in the classroom. During the final semester of many programs, students devote their studio time to creating an architectural project from beginning to end, culminating in a three-dimensional design model.

Most architecture graduates do not become principal designers in architectural firms, and there is some criticism that too much emphasis is placed on the design studio without enough attention given to technical instruction. Others argue that the role of the architecture school is not to develop technical skills but is to provide a broad framework of knowledge and a basic understanding of the desired objectives, realizing that five or six years of formal education cannot provide all the training an architect will need. Nearly everyone working on an architectural project will need to decide what materials to use or how to apply them. Thousands of details must be resolved before the building is completed. To this extent everyone is a designer, and this partly explains the emphasis on design in architecture schools.

A typical architecture program will recognize the importance of graphic skills, and early instruction will be given in freehand drawing and graphic delineation. Various media will be explored, including pencil, ink, color, and often computer graphics. The problem of designing a structure to withstand the forces of gravity, wind, and earthquakes is usually addressed through a series of courses. Beginning with algebra, trigonometry, and physics, most schools require at least one course in calculus and descriptive geometry before the introduction of engineering statics (a development of the study of vector forces from elementary physics). There may be an additional course on structural materials, particularly in engineering-oriented programs. The structures courses may be organized by the structural element (beam, column, etc.) or the structural material (wood, steel, reinforced concrete).

Many schools of architecture offer graduate education for those who have a bachelor's or master's degree in architecture or other areas. Although graduate education beyond the professional degree is not required for practicing architects, it is required for research, teaching, and certain specialties.

SPECIALIZATION

Specialists exist for nearly every aspect of professional practice: programming, specifications, contracts, cost estimating, construction supervision, site planning, interiors, acoustics, lighting, heating and air-conditioning, and electrical and structural design. If you look through the offerings in the catalogs of several academic programs, you will probably find courses covering each of these and other subjects. They may be required or optional or may be integrated into a broader course such as Architectural Technology, Professional Practice, Contract Documents, or Building Systems.

THE PORTFOLIO

Most schools of architecture require a portfolio review as part of the admissions process, whether you are applying directly from high school, from within an undergraduate program, or as a returning graduate student. In all these instances, the strongest portfolios tend to be those that demonstrate the creative potential of the candidate, emphasizing the unique strengths and/or talents the prospective student can bring to the school's program. Whether your talents lie in graphics, design, photography, painting, writing, or any other discipline, approach your portfolio as a design problem and create a presentation that showcases your creativity in a clear and professional manner.

SELECTING A SCHOOL

As mentioned earlier, 117 accredited schools exist in the United States and Canada. It's time to narrow your choices. Your first step should be to obtain a copy of the Association of Collegiate Schools of Architecture (ACSA) publication Guide to Architecture Schools. The guide is available in most architecture libraries and bookstores, and you can order it from the ACSA (see Appendix B). The guide outlines each school's program and explains the basic administrative structure, costs, and enrollment requirements. The listings for ACSA full and candidate member schools describe opportunities and resources available to students, special activities, financial aid, educational philosophy, and programs of study. Choose six possibilities based on a course of study, the geographic region, and whatever other criteria you have set up for your future study. Write or e-mail each school for their college catalogs and other information they might provide. When writing for the college catalogs, ask if the department or school of architecture has specially prepared brochures. You should read these thoroughly before visiting a school.

Talk to other architects about the schools they went to or the schools they'd recommend. Practicing architects are busy but are usually willing to talk to students.

If possible, arrange to visit the schools that interest you. Plan to come when classes are in session so you can talk to various students at different study levels. Walk around the campus and the school of architecture. Get a feel for the environment and if this would be the kind of place where you'd be willing to spend five or six years of your life.

In choosing your program, remember that some mid-list universities may house excellent schools of architecture and famous universities might be the home to only average architecture departments. Of course, make sure the school you choose is accredited by the NAAB or the CACB and that the degree you will receive is an accredited professional degree that fulfills the educational requirement to be eligible for registration. And make sure that course offerings will allow you to focus on any particular interest you have such as design, computers, energy, sustainability, or preservation.

The available financial aid will play a role. Determine if scholarships are an option and if they are based on academic achievement or on need.

Ranking architecture schools is impossible, so asking which is the best school will give you an unsatisfactory answer. Best is best for you. The size, location, cost of living, financial aid, programs offered, and so on will suit you. No school can be excellent in all aspects. In all likelihood, the most important factor in any educational endeavor is your motivation. Most architectural employers are far more interested in what you have accomplished and will continue to accomplish than in the prestige of your degree.

FINANCING YOUR EDUCATION

Cost should not be an automatic deterrent in deciding the program or the number of years you will study because most schools offer financial aid. Though some students may find beginning their college education at a community or junior college a financial necessity, for students who are sure architecture is their chosen career field, the five-year professional degree programs offer excellent opportunities. Students seeking slightly more flexibility should examine five-year programs offering logical curriculum decision points.

Graduate students may receive teaching or research assistantships. For each school you are considering, determine its current tuition and fees, as well as its potential for providing assistance.

The American Institute of Architects (AIA) has minimal scholarship programs applicable to schools in the United States, and local AIA chapters may offer scholarships.

SAMPLE PROGRAMS

The following two programs are chosen only as a sampling to illustrate what is available. Their inclusion here is not intended to be an endorsement, nor is the exclusion of other schools intended to show disapproval.

Pratt Institute
School of Architecture
Brooklyn, New York
Bachelor of Architecture

The Bachelor of Architecture program is an accredited program requiring a minimum of five years of study. The 175 credits required for the Bachelor of Architecture degree are organized in three main categories: a core of required courses in architectural study, liberal arts courses, and electives. The core of ninety-eight credits is primarily taken in the first three years and is designed to give basic professional preparation in architectural design, construction, technology, graphic communication, and the humanistic aspects of design.

The liberal arts area requires forty-five credits, of which nine credits are taken within the School of Architecture (Architecture 206, Architecture 207, Architecture 308), six credits in English, six credits in cultural history, six credits in science, and six credits in social science. The remaining twelve credits are taken as electives from among the liberal arts courses offered by the School of Liberal Arts and Sciences.

The elective courses are composed of eighteen credits of professional electives selected from courses offered by the School of Architecture's undergraduate and graduate programs and of fourteen all-Institute electives, which may be selected from courses offered by any school in the institute. By selecting courses within all elective areas during later semesters, students can develop their own unique architectural education in accord with their own needs and goals. Individual curricula may be developed to place more emphasis on such subject areas as advocacy planning, building technology, history and theory, planning, construction management, and urban design.

The degree project year completes the student's academic architectural experience with an in-depth design study, preceded and accompanied by research. The degree project is executed with critics of the student's choice.

Options combining the undergraduate degree with various master's degrees are also available in architecture, planning, and urban design. For more information visit www.pratt.edu/school_of_architecture.

University of Manitoba
Department of Architecture
Winnipeg, Manitoba, Canada
Architecture and City Planning

The program combines academic and technical studies to provide students with an understanding of the technology used in the making of built human environments, knowledge and understanding of the interrelationships between natural and the built environments, an understanding of human factors as they shape the design and construction of built environments, and an ability to use visual information and graphic communications and understand spatial analysis in constructing human environments.

The curriculum is structured around a design studio with four study areas:

1. A central core of design, design theory, and graphics
2. Cultural and environmental history
3. Building technology and environmental controls
4. Electives in the humanities, social sciences, and the natural sciences

The design core provides opportunities for students to demonstrate comprehension of knowledge and skills acquired in all four study areas. Students spend ten to twelve contact hours a week in design studios, resolving problems that vary in context from the analysis of a simple natural object to community spaces and complex urban problems. Students select an area of specialization such as the Architecture, Landscape Architecture, or City Planning option in their third year, which qualifies them for application to those graduate programs. The program is one of the more demanding undergraduate courses of study at the University of Manitoba, in terms of contact hours and the time required for completing design and other assignments outside class hours. Consequently, good work habits and a mature and responsible personality are definite assets. Students must learn to budget time so they do not neglect other course work requirements.

The department sets exacting standards for attendance and academic design performance. Its graduates are highly rated among practicing professionals in architecture, city planning, and landscape architecture, as well as other professional design academic programs of study in North America. The Bachelor of Environmental Design (BED) program within the Faculty of Architecture is not specifically concerned with pollution, ecology, biological, or chemical environmental problems. If your interests are in these areas, Environmental Science in the Faculty of Science would be more appropriate. For more information, visit umanitoba.ca/faculties/architecture/programs/edesign/environmental_design.htm.

STUDENT STATISTICS

According to the NAAB, 12,221 students were enrolled full-time in B.Arch. accredited programs and 1,127 students were enrolled part-time across the United States in 2006. Full-time M.Arch. candidates totaled 5,664, and there were 656 part-time master's-level students. Of these totals, 7,888 were women, 1,150 were African-American students, 121 were Native American students, 1,526 were Asian/Pacific Isle students, and 2,222 were Hispanic students.

SKILLS AN ARCHITECT MUST HAVE

Architects must be able to communicate their ideas visually to clients. Artistic and drawing ability helps but is not essential. More important are a visual orientation and the ability to conceptualize and understand spatial relationships. Verbal and written communication skills, the ability to work independently or as part of a team, and creativity are important qualities for anyone becoming an architect. Computer literacy is required as most firms use computers for writing specifications, two-dimensional and three-dimensional drafting, and financial management. A knowledge of computer-aided design and drafting (CADD) is helpful and will become essential as architectural firms continue to adopt this technology. Recently, the profession recognized National CAD Standards (NCS). Architecture students who master the NCS will have an advantage in the job market.

TRAINING PERIODS

All state architectural registration boards require a training period before candidates may sit for the ARE and become licensed. Many states have adopted the training standards established by the Intern Development Program (IDP), a branch of the AIA and the National Council of Architectural Registration Boards (NCARB). These standards stipulate broad and diversified training under the supervision of a licensed architect over a three-year period. (Additional information on the IDP is provided later in this chapter.) Graduates with degrees in architecture enter related fields such as graphic, interior, or industrial design; urban planning; real estate development; civil engineering; or construction management. In such cases, an architectural license and, thus, the internship period are not required.

During a training period leading up to licensing as architects, entry-level workers are called intern-architects. This training period, which generally lasts three years, allows for practical work experience and a paycheck and prepares the intern-architect for the ARE. Typical intern duties may include preparing construction drawings on CADD or assisting in the design of one part of a project.

ARCHITECT REGISTRATION EXAMINATION (ARE)

After completing the internship period, intern-architects are eligible to sit for the ARE. The examination tests candidates on architectural knowledge and is given in sections throughout the year. Candidates who pass the ARE and meet all standards established by their state board are licensed to practice in that state. After becoming licensed and gaining experience, architects take on more duties and manage entire projects. In large firms, architects may advance to supervisory or managerial positions. Some architects become partners in established firms, and others set up their own practice.

Several states require continuing education to maintain a license, and more states are expected to adopt mandatory continuing education. Requirements vary by state but usually involve the completion of a certain number of credits every year or two through seminars, workshops, formal university classes, conferences, self-study courses, or other sources.

PREPARING EARLY

If you're still in high school while investigating this career, you can prepare by giving yourself a solid background in the physical sciences, including mathematics. You should also be able to conceptualize at an above-average level, have a strong proficiency in oral and written communication, demonstrate a wide interest in the humanities, and be able to draw and sketch with ease. It is doubtful any high school student would be able to master all skill areas, but even a few skills makes a good start. Drawing is probably the most easily acquired skill and math sometimes the most difficult. A good course in freehand drawing would ultimately prove more valuable than drafting, and one semester of drafting is probably enough.

Most architecture programs assume entering students have had at least trigonometry and one physics course in high school. Surprisingly, the majority of professional architects are not highly proficient in mathematical skills, and those who are (and are strong in structural design) often possess a lower than average ability in drawing or design skills.

Architecture is a diversified, multifaceted profession, with many opportunities for specialization. Even if you do not excel in math, drawing, or writing, you may still become an outstanding architect. If you spot a weakness in your preparation, do not worry but give it your attention. Overall, the architecture school is probably more interested in your class rank, national test scores, and general aptitude than specific courses or skills.

High School Courses to Take

Geography, English, drawing, history, philosophy, and government are useful to everyone. Botany is highly recommended for those planning to pursue landscape architecture. Foreign languages are not often required in architecture programs, but most will accept a language as an elective. With opportunities for study abroad, the right language can have considerable practical use even before graduation, and ease with other languages can be valuable in the study of architectural history and the conduct of research. For those working for firms with international contacts and contracts, another language would be a plus. A course in industrial arts can be helpful. Speech or debate classes are important because architects and architecture students must often express or explain complex ideas orally.

In general, architecture schools expect their students to have above-average intelligence. They want you to be eager to learn and be both self-motivated and self-disciplined with a broad range of interests.

Summer Work Experience During High School

A summer job in building construction is useful and sometimes easier to find than a job in a professional architectural firm. If no related jobs are available, make the public library your second home and study books and magazines on architecture as much as possible. A common deficiency of many architecture students who perform below the average is a lack of interest in reading. Address that deficiency before starting your professional degree.

Architecture Schools: Special Programs

To provide additional insight into the typical course of study in architecture, many institutions have programs for high school students interested in architectural studies. These programs, usually lasting for several weeks, are designed to be microcosms of the way you will study architecture within a university curriculum. Going through one of these programs may help dispel misconceptions about what architects do and how they learn to do it. ACSA annually publishes a list of summer programs as part of a publication titled Architecture Schools: Special Programs. (See Appendix B for more information.)

INTERN DEVELOPMENT PROGRAM (IDP)

The IDP is a joint program of the AIA, NCARB, and ACSA. Currently, all states except Arizona require IDP training for initial registration.

The IDP addresses the participant's professional development needs by providing a wide range of resources. The IDP training requirement establishes levels of experience in important areas of architectural practice. Through the IDP mentorship system, you receive advice and guidance from practitioners. The IDP record-keeping system facilitates the documentation of internship activities, while the IDP supplementary education system provides a variety of learning resources designed to enrich training.

Many of those who have participated in the IDP found they performed significantly better on the ARE, received relevant and comprehensive preparation for the profession, and developed valuable skills and competencies. In addition, students gained credit for nontraditional work—this is a great way to explore careers in architecture and became eligible for a possible deferment of National Direct Student Loan (NDSL) and Guaranteed Student Loan (GSL) educational loans.

As a student participating in the IDP, you may benefit from the informed counsel of experienced practitioners. You may apply work experience toward registration board training requirements after the third year in a B.Arch. or four-plus-two M.Arch. program, and after the first year in a three- or four-year M.Arch. program. You can document your progress through an IDP council record. This provides for periodic review of your progress, reduces the time and paperwork needed to apply for registration, becomes part of your portfolio, and documents your versatility to prospective employers. You can plan your work experience using the IDP core competencies to map out the skills and knowledge you need to establish yourself as a competent practitioner.

To get involved, contact your school's IDP educator coordinator (usually one of the professional practice faculty), or call the AIA and request its IDP guidelines and an application for an NCARB council record. Contact your state registration board and request a copy of the registration requirements.

Apply for your NCARB council record. Students and recent graduates (up to six months from graduation) can apply for $100 instead of paying the full fee. The balance of the fee is deferred until you are eligible to take the ARE.

Contact local interns who are involved in the IDP to establish a mentor relationship while you are still attending school. They can advise you on how to exploit your internship, improve your portfolio presentation and job-finding skills, and investigate firms and wages.

Attend job fairs, firm presentations, and career development lectures sponsored by your AIA chapters. This will help you learn more about local firms so you can target the ones you like. Establish a time line for when you want to become licensed. This will help you establish goals and deadlines.

Review the quality of your internship. If your firm does not have an annual review system, ask your employer and coworkers to evaluate your progress.

Discuss your goals and IDP training expectations for the upcoming year with your mentor. Evaluate how your present firm is helping to achieve your personal and professional goals.

Contact your state registration board to learn about the registration requirements. Verify the ARE application process and deadlines. Review the IDP guidelines and compare the IDP requirements with your state's registration requirements. Contact the NCARB and your state registration board to clarify your questions and concerns.

Keep your portfolio current. Maintain a daily log of training units in conjunction with your time sheet. Review the IDP core competencies and divide your hours worked into the proper training areas to help expedite your IDP training reports.

Talk with other interns. Find out about their firms' projects and share your internship experiences.

INTERN DEVELOPMENT PROGRAM (IDP) CORE COMPETENCIES

The AIA, in conjunction with NCARB, has identified the core competencies necessary to measure an individual's ability to practice in the architectural profession. Thus, the IDP is recognized by a majority of states' licensing authorities as a necessary element in the education of graduates of schools of architecture to be qualified to take the exam for licensure. The following represent two sample core competencies required by the IDP. (A listing of free information about IDP training and other topics of interest can be downloaded from ncarb.org/IDP/resources.html.)

Building Cost Analysis

Building cost analysis involves the estimation of a project's probable construction cost. At the completion of your internship, you should be able to do the following:

- Analyze and evaluate construction costs
- Prepare a building cost analysis that meets the program's requirements and provides alternatives for the owner or client
- Prepare preliminary cost analyses using unit cost/building type basis (cost per square foot) and unit cost basis (material labor)

- Investigate and prepare quantity calculations for selected materials
- Research life-cycle cost information in relation to specifications
- Factor the current inflation rate and other economic variables into the cost estimates

Schematic Design

Schematic design involves the development of graphic alternative solutions to the program for the client's approval. At the completion of your internship, you should be able to develop alternative solutions to a specific program and document and present your solutions to a client for selection and approval.

In addition to these core competencies, you will have to have the following skills:

- Develop a project's program into alternative conceptual design proposals
- Evaluate engineering systems appropriate to the project
- Prepare volume and area calculations and evaluate the cost of alternative design proposals
- Prepare presentation drawings and models
- Review the schematic design with the client and revise the design based on the client's feedback
- Communicate the intent of the design orally, graphically, and in writing to facilitate the client's decision-making process
- Coordinate the consultants' activities relative to the schematic design
- Incorporate relevant code requirements into the schematic design

If, upon graduation from architecture school, you accomplish these and other core competencies required by the IDP, you will be ready for licensure and the practice of architecture.

CHAPTER 3

RESIDENTIAL, COMMERCIAL, AND INSTITUTIONAL ARCHITECTURE

In 2006 architects held about 132,000 jobs across the United States. The majority of jobs are in architectural firms, most of which employ fewer than five workers. A few architects work for general building contractors or for government agencies responsible for housing, planning, or community development, such as the U.S. Departments of Defense and the Interior and the General Services Administration. About three in ten architects are self-employed.

Architects design a wide variety of buildings, including office and apartment buildings, schools, libraries, churches, factories, hospitals and health-care facilities, private residences, and airport terminals. They design complexes such as urban centers, college campuses, industrial parks, and entire communities. They may advise on the selection of building sites, prepare cost analysis and land-use studies, and do long-range planning for land development.

SPECIALIZING

Architects sometimes specialize in one phase of work. Some specialize in the design of one type of building, for example, hospitals, schools, or individual houses. Others focus on planning and predesign services or construction management and do little design work.

Architects often work with engineers, urban planners, interior designers, landscape architects, and others. (These related fields are discussed in later chapters.)

In this chapter, we will focus on firsthand accounts from architects doing residential, commercial, and institutional work. First, here are a few sample job listings to give you an idea of what's out there. Because these are meant only as examples, hiring firms are not mentioned. You may find similar current listings by visiting the American Institute of Architects (AIA) website at aiaonline.com or by conducting your own Internet search using keywords such as architecture and jobs.

SAMPLE JOB LISTINGS

Architect/Designer, Wisconsin

A design firm is offering positions for passionate, ambitious graduates, with two to three years' minimum architectural experience, to work on all phases of single and multifamily residential, mixed-use commercial, institutional, and urban design projects.

Project Manager/Interiors, Colorado

An innovative and award-winning 160-person architecture and interiors firm is seeking talented individuals for exciting large-scale projects with high-tech firms that are pushing the boundaries of traditional corporate architecture and redefining the work environment. An excellent opportunity to work in a collaborative atmosphere that advocates "whole building" thinking. Upcoming projects include corporate campuses that incorporate recreational facilities, restaurants, and shopping to create independent communities. Qualifications: five to seven years of experience; AutoCAD 13/14 2D proficiency preferred; excellent organizational skills; degree in interior design or architecture; interior design certification or architectural license preferred.

Architect, Missouri

Must be licensed and have three to five years' experience as architect. Position involves all aspects of health-care design and construction. Must have verbal and writing skills and have working knowledge of AutoCAD 14 or 2000. Presentation skills preferred. Salary negotiable.

Forensic Architect, Oregon
National construction consulting firm seeking architect specializing in forensic investigation, construction defect litigation, and code interpretation. Comprehensive salary and benefits package offered.

Intermediate-Senior Level Architect, Texas
Architects with six to fifteen years' experience for quality community, recreation, library, and resort projects. Candidates must have general experience in architectural design, strong technical skills, and detailing expertise with AutoCAD 14. Applicants must be responsive learners and strong team players. Intermediate technical staff is needed for preparation of design development and construction documents for Type-II and Type-V projects ranging from $3–50 million. Previous work in related project and building types and 3-D modeling a plus.

Library Architect, Washington
Library architect with five-plus years' experience in design, production, or project management of community or academic library projects to work in our expanding library practice. Candidate must have strong communication as well as graphic skills, experience leading design or production teams, and experience working with public and/or academic community user groups. Work experience must include strong technical, CAD, and teamwork skills. Previous work in related community or academic building types will be considered.

Staff Architect, Ohio
Immediate opportunity for a staff architect to help take a project from design development through construction. We specialize in designing and building prestigious senior retirement communities; therefore, we would appreciate health-care experience. Proficiency in AutoCAD 14 is required, as is a professional degree with at least one year of experience. Registration is a plus, not a requirement.

FIRSTHAND ACCOUNTS

Joel André, Architect

Joel André is an architect and interior designer and owns his own firm called André Marquez Architects, located in Virginia Beach, Virginia. He has been practicing architecture since 1979, when he graduated from the School of Architecture at Pratt Institute in Brooklyn, New York. He has a Bachelor of Architecture degree.

In 1988, he passed the New York state licensing boards and became a licensed architect in the state of New York and, through reciprocity, acquired his Virginia license, allowing him to practice in Virginia.

Getting Started

"I became interested in this profession after being exposed to it by an uncle who was an architect. So, from a young age, I can remember wanting to do what he did. As it turns out, between all the cousins and distant cousins, six others are architects and engineers in my family.

"I have always been fascinated with the ability to design a structure that will meet a specific human need. I have always enjoyed the problem-solving aspect of the profession.

"I got my first job in the profession when I came out of school, working for a local architect in New York who had also graduated from Pratt. It was a small firm specializing in renovation and use conversion in New York, but primarily in Park Slope, Brooklyn, which is a brownstone type of neighborhood that was in the process of becoming gentrified.

"The wonderful thing about working in this firm was that because it was so small, from the beginning, I was able to get involved with the actual design of projects and be exposed to every facet of the profession.

"Some of the people I graduated with followed a different track. They went to large firms, where they were exposed to larger or more prominent projects, but did not get, in my opinion, the full exposure to the nuts and bolts of the business that I got as fast as I got it. In the larger firms your growth is a bit slower, but the advantage is that you get to work on some major projects. There are pros and cons in either track.

"Four years ago, I was in transition out of a position as a project architect in a firm in Virginia Beach, when I decided to take the plunge and start my own firm. Because of the relationships that I had in the profession and past clients I had remained in contact with, I was able to open my doors and hang my shingle without too much struggle. Because the firm I was working for closed its doors, there was no conflict in servicing some of their old clients. Like all new businesses, we go through some tight times, but on the average, we are doing better than would be expected."

What the Work Is Like

"Our clients include commercial, residential, churches, the Department of Defense, as well as state and municipal organizations. Because of our client diversity, the types of projects that we are involved with also tend to be varied. That makes the day-to-day aspect of the business interesting. But the bottom line of this profession is that it is a service-oriented field. It requires a desire to serve people because, ultimately, most buildings that you will be involved in designing will be used by people to facilitate or meet a specific need."

A Typical Project

"To give you a broad-brush look at the practice of architecture, let me first run through the process for a typical project:

"One of the indispensable facets of the business of architecture is marketing. This involves following leads on who is planning to build or even earlier, who is thinking of building. If you do work for the state or federal government, this involves responding to requests for proposals (RFPs) published in special publications or advertised in the local papers.

"Once you respond to the advertisement requesting architectural services, a selection process occurs since several architectural firms pursue these ads.

"Assuming you are selected, you negotiate a contract with the client, establishing the scope of the project and your fee for the services you will provide. The contracts establish the schedule in which the construction documents will be accomplished. These documents include the drawings, specifications, and the coordination of the other disciplines involved in the project.

"Generally, these are other engineering fields, such as civil engineers for the site work, structural engineers for the foundations and structure framework of the building, the plumbing and the mechanical—

meaning heating and air-conditioning—electrical engineers, landscape architects, fire protection engineer for sprinkler systems, and any other disciplines for the special conditions requiring input, such as acoustics or lighting.

"The architect is responsible for the production of the documents that will be used by the builder or contractor to build the building. He is responsible for making sure the program or the list of requirements and needs and functions the building has to meet satisfies all the needs of the owner/user, from a functional point of view as well as for the safety and welfare of the occupants.

"He must do all of this within budget, which often requires a reevaluation of the scope of the project to fit the budget or an adjustment of the budget to fit the scope. This must occur in the project's beginning stages. You may design a great building, but if it can't be built because it exceeds the budget it is a bad experience for everyone. So, an important facet of this business is cost estimating.

"Once the scope and budget for the project have been reconciled and the architect has pulled together our team of consultants, we launch into the project's concept design phase. This is where the preliminary design work is done. We establish the general direction of the shape, volume, basic space layouts, and site layout, showing where on the site the building will sit. We consider access, visibility, street presentation, relationship to neighbors, solar orientation, site drainage, utility connections, the building's appearance, and materials usage, while complying with all the zoning and building codes.

"During this phase and all the other phases of this process, we do a constant review of the cost and budget to ensure the decisions being made in the design process are going to be buildable.

"Once the client has reviewed and approved the concept design (this can require several presentations and revisions), the project goes into the design development phase. This is where we refine the design, select the materials, give directions to the engineer consultants, and coordinate the various disciplines.

"At the end of this phase, we finalize the building design and evaluate the cost versus budget.

"From here, we proceed to the construction document production phase. We create the construction drawings or blueprints, as well as the specifications that detail the materials and their quality, installation, maintenance, and warranties.

"The specifications complement the drawings to give the contractor all the information he will need to build the building as it is designed. This phase generally is the longest.

"While the architect is producing his drawings and specifications, his consultants are producing their drawings and documents that will complement the architectural documents. We add them to the architectural drawing set, and we add their respective specification sections to the project specification book.

"Once we complete the construction documents, they are released so contractors can make their bids. Once we have selected a contractor, the architect must ensure the client is getting what he is paying for and that the contractor is using the materials and installing the equipment specified in the construction documents. At the same time, the architect has a responsibility to the contractor to ensure he has all the information he needs to do his work.

"Once the building is completed and all systems are operational, the project is closed out, and the owner/user assumes occupancy of the building. Ideally, all parties are satisfied and we all part friends. This, I find, depends greatly on the individual players in this complex process. However, we do carry liability insurance.

"Generally, there are no typical days. Depending on which phase of a project we are in, we have specific goals we are working toward. It gets more interesting when we have several projects in various phases of development. This is where a good staff of designers, CAD operators, administrative staff, and project architects and project managers come into play.

"Depending on the types of projects you do, the approach to the work might vary. Some firms specialize in one building type, such as hospitals or hotels or residential.

"However, on the average, because of my position, I spend a lot of time coordinating the work that goes on in the office between the client, consultants, contractors, and all other interested parties. I do the concept design for the projects. I want that initial input, establishing the direction of the design to the satisfaction of the client.

"This is a people profession. If my client is unhappy, I am going to be unhappy since the client will find himself or herself another architect."

Upsides and Downsides

"The upside of architecture is that it is a profession that will give you a view on your environment different from most other professions. I like the creative aspect most about practicing architecture. The design and problem-solving aspects are what I like to do. I love to design and conceptualize a client's vision into a product that fulfills that vision. I enjoy working out the details in the design development phase. Unfortunately, that is only about 10 to 15 percent of the whole process.

"I enjoy the construction document phase of the work, the working drawings and the specifications, but not as much as the design.

"The part I enjoy the least is the administrative or business end of the profession. That was not why I became an architect, but it is an unavoidable part of the business. I would suggest that an M.B.A. would be an ideal postgraduate degree for architects. Either that or hire a good business manager. We have to wear so many hats as architects, so trying to wing it as a businessperson can be deadly.

"I find that architecture affects every aspect of your life because it does require a love for the profession to remain in it."

Advice from Joel André

"The primary requisites to be an architect are a good understanding of the profession and a love for the work. I say that because it does require a lot from you, often with small rewards, especially in the beginning.

"The qualities you'll need to be a good architect are good people skills, problem-solving skills, creativity, and an appreciation of the pure logic of engineering.

"For training, I would recommend a five-year school providing a professional degree, and practical office work during summer and winter breaks. Find an architect who will bring you in and maintain that relationship throughout your schooling. It's an incredible asset to have the right expectations of the profession when you come out of school, as opposed to stepping into the reality of everyday practice while your head is still in the clouds of academia.

"To get started, I recommend you visit an architect's office or, better yet, several offices, and if at all possible, spend a couple of weeks of a summer vacation while in your sophomore or junior year in an architect's office, even if you have to volunteer your time. Then I would visit some architectural schools to get a good understanding of the profession.

"Ultimately, make sure it's something you want to do and understand the sacrifices it will require."

Judy Moore, Architect

Judy Moore is a self-employed architect (Judy Moore & Associates) in Albuquerque, New Mexico. She's involved in residential and commercial projects and has been in the field since 1989. She earned her B.A. in architecture from the University of New Mexico.

Getting Started

"Originally, I was an art major (sculpture) but felt the competition too steep and the opportunities too few to make a go of it. I switched my major to architecture because it would be easier to support myself and I felt that there was a strong enough connection to sculpture to keep my creativity satisfied.

"I started doing residential remodel jobs when I was a sophomore in college to help pay for my education. The first few jobs were for relatives and friends of relatives. They did not pay much, but the clients were patient with me and I appreciated the opportunities to learn the things that would have been unavailable to me through school.

"I started my own business in 1989 doing contract work for larger architectural firms and some residential projects for myself."

What the Work Is Like

"The residential work I do includes new construction (custom homes) and remodeling jobs, large and small. The commercial jobs include medical facilities, schools, and resorts/hotels.

"Currently, I am contracting work for a company that designs, builds, and remodels resort areas around the world. Each project has a five- or six-member team assigned to it. Each team travels to the particular job site to gather information for the preliminary design development phase (usually five to seven days, depending on the location).

"My duties vary from team to team and job to job. Most of the time I am the person responsible for preparing the construction documents for obtaining the building permits.

"During the project, I participate in design development. I attend a weekly staff meeting during which each team provides an update for its particular project. Each week, I also attend at least one team meeting for my project. During these meetings, we deal with unforeseen problems, and we review and sometimes revise our schedules to meet or change target dates for each project phase.

"Most of the time my work day is too short. I could use a couple more hours, since the time passes quickly. I enjoy the work, and some weeks I work forty hours, some sixty hours, depending on deadlines."

The Upsides and Downsides

"One of the things I've always liked about being an architect is learning about the specific uses and needs of each project, from playgrounds for handicapped children to hotels. Each project provides an opportunity to learn about the facilities and the people who work or live in them. Each comes with a set of design criteria that must be researched and developed.

"I enjoy the challenge of developing designs that meet the clients' goals and needs, while remaining within the constraints of a budget, the building codes, and the geographical site and its surroundings for the structure.

"Some of the things I like and dislike about my job are the same. On larger projects, I like it that someone else deals with the clients and manages the money. On smaller projects, I like dealing directly with the clients and managing the money myself.

"Small projects often involve working closely with people wanting to build something they need (a spare room for an elderly parent needing home care, or a remodel of an outdated kitchen). Their budgets are small, and for that reason, I usually adjust my fee accordingly (to a point).

"Larger projects involve clients with larger budgets who are used to dealing with professionals and are willing to spend the money needed to get what they want.

"Each type of project, large and small, requires finding design solutions for specific problems, which is what I like to do. I like it because I'm good at it. It's easy to like something you're good at."

Advice from Judy Moore

"If you are considering pursuing architecture as a career, you should enjoy the process of design and feel good about or proud of your solutions.

"There are no monetary guarantees. This profession, like many others, moves up and down with the economy. It is a tight community whose jobs depend on referrals and word-of-mouth and being in the right place at the right time."

Julie Haney, Architect

Julie Haney is a project architect with Ridge Builders Group, a design/build firm in Davis, California. She works with residential remodels and custom homes.

She earned her B.Arch. at California Polytechnic State University in San Luis Obispo, California, and has been working in the field since 1990.

Getting Started

"I was really interested in art and math and wanted to combine the two, so architecture was a perfect fit. I felt that since I had to work for a living I wanted to do something that I enjoyed."

What the Work Is Like

"As a project architect in a design/build firm I experience every level of architecture, from the initial site visit/measurement meeting with the client, to the final walk-through at the end of the job.

"It is very rewarding to experience the sprouting of an idea all the way through to a physical, three-dimensional realization of that idea, especially when the client is thrilled beyond his or her dreams.

"To achieve this, though, a lot must happen. There are two main parts: design and construction. Within the design part are three basic phases: programming and schematics, design development, and construction documentation.

"Phase one is where I meet with the client and review with him or her the estimate letter that outlines the project. (This was previously generated by one of our estimators.) Because I mostly work on remodels, I discuss the likes and dislikes of the existing situation or house with the client. The process evolves as I take the newly gathered information and turn it into a schematic design for the client to approve. This schematic design is a springboard for generating ideas and narrowing it into the final idea.

"Once the final schematic is approved, phase two starts, which is design development. During this phase, the design is further developed, window and door sizes are established, as are the exterior elevations and general material selections. A midproject estimate at this time is a good idea for a reality check on project costs. The end of phase two is marked by the design being developed to the point where the drawings and plans can go out to consultants for structural and Title 24 analysis (California energy code).

"During the time the plans are at the consultants, I continue meeting with the client to specify finish materials, plumbing, lighting fixtures, appliances, and so on.

"I develop details, and once the drawings come back from the consultants, I incorporate all details and consultant work into the final set of drawings. The client reviews this, and it goes to the building department for plan check. The specifications are completed and given to the estimator along with a copy of the plans so that he or she can finalize the construction costs. This marks the end of phase three.

"After this, I respond to plan check comments, attend a preconstruction meeting at the start of the remodel job, review shop drawings from the cabinetmaker, and make general site observations."

The Upsides and Downsides

"I like the various job tasks I do. I love specifying finish materials and coming up with designs. I love seeing the final project, as well as seeing the project grow. I love when my clients stand in awe and say, 'this project is so wonderful that it has changed the quality my life.'

"But I hate indecisive clients who change their minds every day, clients who get upset and don't know how to be civil when discussing their issues, or clients who expect me to read their mind and then get mad because I didn't foresee their inability to visualize after they claimed they completely understood their plans and specs."

Advice from Julie Haney

"The main skills for an apprentice architect to develop are computer drafting, 3-D visualization, people and communication skills, the ability to sketch your ideas clearly and simply, and business sense.

"Obviously, education is the key here. Go to a reputable school that has a solid program or specializes in a field you are interested in. Especially look for a school that teaches commonsense thinking.

"I strongly recommend working in an architecture office during summer breaks or vacations. Most schools don't teach how to complete a full set of working drawings or other basics. They mostly concentrate on design and other useful things.

"You will have to take a battery of tests to become licensed after you graduate. Local AIA chapters can help guide you on this process.

"The job outlook depends on what field you are thinking about. If you are into designing elderly care facilities, you will find lots of opportunities as the baby boomers age.

"Remodels have to continue to be plentiful as land becomes more precious. Community-oriented neighborhoods would be a great thing to see more of, especially if they are sustainable.

"Careers in solar and energy-efficient building design would have the greatest impact on the quality of the environment and future generations. But as professors have told our classes, 'if you are in architecture for the money, get out of here and go to the business department.'

"As architects, we are partly responsible for the built environment and how it impacts our natural resources as well as the human psyche. You should not take this big responsibility lightly. And through our creations, we can make a difference."

HISTORIC PRESERVATION

Restoration architects, or architects specializing in historic preservation, have much of a general architect's experience. They understand how to plan spaces, organize construction materials, and assemble construction documents.

The difference between general architects and restoration architects is that the latter's work experience has primarily focused on historic buildings. In addition, restoration architects have a specialized knowledge and understanding of federal, state, and local regulations with regard to historic preservation. They will know the standards set by the particular style of architecture.

PRESERVATION CATEGORIES

Preservation includes several categories. Adaptive reuse is when architects provide a new function for older structures that would otherwise be demolished. For example, a defunct mill is converted into an office building or a college. Architectural conservation involves using special techniques to halt further deterioration of building materials. Restoration, which may be called historical restoration, involves the meticulous return of a building to its former appearance at a particular period in history. Rehabilitation or renovation involves altering or upgrading existing buildings and structures.

RELATED FIELDS

Careers in historic preservation include architectural conservators, architectural historians, curators of structures, and other preservationists, who all share a love of historic buildings and architecture. They might specialize in a particular period or style, fascinated by Victorian gingerbread, strong red brick or federal woodwork, and old frame farmhouses and barns. Most, however, are generalists, possessing knowledge that crosses the centuries. These professionals are good researchers or artists and have strong organizational skills and an interest in the environment as well as history.

ARCHITECTURAL CONSERVATORS

Architectural conservators are not necessarily registered architects. They might have started out in the construction and contracting field, gaining along the way specialized technical experience in problems that occur with historic buildings. Some of these problems involve the historic building fabric such as cracks in foundations and walls, water seepage, and the cleaning of buildings. They understand how buildings were constructed during earlier periods and know what kinds of complications result from the natural course of time and different climatic and environmental conditions. They are familiar with building materials, roofs, windows, exterior cladding, and various construction types, such as wood frame or masonry-clad structures. Architectural conservators are also sometimes known as curators of structures.

ARCHITECTURAL HISTORIANS

Architectural historians are historians with an interest in architecture. They are generally not registered architects. They often work with restoration architects, however, conducting specialized investigations and performing all the research necessary to get a restoration project underway. They dig up a building's history: when it was constructed, what its original purpose was, how long it was vacant, whether any changes had been made. They assemble a historic structures report for the architects who want to make their restoration work as accurate as possible.

Architectural historians can work in academic settings, for private architectural firms, and for government agencies concerned with historic preservation. The minimum educational requirement for an architectural historian is an undergraduate degree in history or architectural history, though most positions require a graduate degree.

HISTORIC INTERIOR DESIGNERS

To achieve authenticity, the interior of a historic building must be given as much attention as the exterior, especially if the building will be used as a museum open to the public. Historic interior designers can be architects or specially trained professionals. They must be experienced in the investigation, documentation, research, and analysis of the lighting, furnishings, finishes, and decorative arts of building interiors. Historic interior specialists generally work as part of a team with the restoration architect and conservator.

ASSOCIATIONS INVOLVED WITH HISTORIC PRESERVATION

The following organizations are listed here because their work involves historic preservation. They depend on membership to survive and encourage anyone with an interest to join. They provide jobs to restoration architects.

National Trust for Historic Preservation (National Trust)

The National Trust is a nonprofit organization, chartered by Congress in 1949, now with more than 250,000 individual members. It is dedicated to protecting the irreplaceable. It fights to save historic buildings and the neighborhoods and landscapes they anchor. The National Trust's mission is to preserve and revitalize the livability of our communities by leading the nation in saving America's historic environments. It provides technical advice and financial assistance to nonprofit organizations and public agencies engaged in preservation and to the general public. The National Trust advocates for protection of the country's heritage in the courts and with legislative and regulatory agencies.

Through education and advocacy, the National Trust is revitalizing communities and is challenging citizens to create sensible plans for the future. It has six regional offices, twenty historic sites, and works with thousands of local community groups nationwide. Most of the National Trust's funding comes from membership dues, corporation and foundation grants, endowment income, and merchandise sales. About 22 percent comes from a matching grant awarded by the U.S. Congress through the U.S. Department of the Interior. The National Trust believes that the employment outlook in the historic preservation field has grown dramatically over the past decade. Its concerns have enlarged from a relatively small number of historic sites, museums, and buildings to historic neighborhoods, commercial districts, and rural landscapes.

The growing sophistication of the field is reflected in the greater diversity of professionals who contribute to preservation work. Historians, curators, and other museum professionals have joined forces with architects, lawyers, designers, realtors, planners, developers, mortgage lenders, and others. Once found working only in museums, libraries, and historical societies, preservationists are employed in real estate firms that specialize in historical properties and in financial institutions that invest in older neighborhoods.

The National Trust employs many specialists in its national office in Washington and in its seven regional offices. In addition, the National Trust owns and operates eighteen historic house museums. It publishes *Historic Preservation* magazine and *Historic Preservation News*, which it distributes to members. The latter lists job opportunities and internships within the National Trust and outside organizations.

For more information, write to the following address:

National Trust for Historic Preservation
1785 Massachusetts Ave. NW
Washington, DC 20036
nationaltrust.org

U.S. Artifacts Recovery Group (USARA) (with the National Association for the Preservation of Historical Artifacts)

By connecting with other associations, individuals, government agencies, and others, the USARA feels it can save more history (together with the National Association for the Preservation of Historical Artifacts) than by doing it alone.

The combined mission statement is "to bridge the gaps in the present preservation efforts, and assist individuals, corporations, local, state, and federal government agencies."

For more information, visit angelfire.com/nc/usaa/index.html.

The Association for Preservation Technology International (APTI)

The APTI is a multidisciplinary organization dedicated to "advancing the application of technology to the conservation of the built environment." APTI members include architects, conservators, consultants, contractors, craftspersons, curators, developers, educators, engineers, historians, landscape architects, managers, planners, preservationists, technicians, tradespeople, and others involved in the systematic application of the knowledge of methods and materials to the conservation of buildings, districts, and artifacts.

For more information, write to the following address:

Association for Preservation Technology International
3085 Stevenson Dr., Suite 200
Springfield, IL 62703
apti.org

International Council on Monuments and Sites (ICOMOS)

ICOMOS is an international nongovernmental organization of professionals, dedicated to the conservation of the world's historic monuments and sites. The U.S. National Committee of ICOMOS (US/ICOMOS) fosters heritage conservation and historic preservation at the national and international levels through education and training, international exchange of people and information, technical assistance, documentation, advocacy, and other activities consistent with the goals of ICOMOS and through collaboration with other organizations.

US/ICOMOS membership includes professionals, practitioners, supporters, and organizations committed to the protection, preservation, and conservation of the world's cultural heritage. ICOMOS is UNESCO's principal advisor in matters concerning the conservation and protection of monuments and sites. With the World Conservation Union (IUCN), ICOMOS has an international role under the World Heritage Convention to advise the World Heritage Committee and UNESCO on the nomination of new sites to the World Heritage List.

Through its sixteen International Scientific Committees of experts from around the world and through its triennial General Assembly, ICOMOS seeks to establish international standards for the preservation, restoration, and management of the cultural environment. Many of these standards have been promulgated as Charters by the organization as a result of adoption by the ICOMOS General Assembly. ICOMOS activities are governed by a set of statutes that were adopted by the Fifth General Assembly in Moscow on May 22, 1978.

For more information, write to the following addresses:

ICOMOS International Secretariat
49-51, rue de la Fédération
75015 Paris
France
international.icomos.org

U.S. National Committee of the ICOMOS
401 F St. NW, Suite 331
Washington, DC 20001
icomos.org/usicomos

Federal Highway Administration (FHWA)

The FHWA has an awards program for preservation projects, particularly for historic bridges. The National Historic Covered Bridge Preservation (NHCBP) program was established by Section 1224 of the Transportation Equity Act for the 21st Century (TEA-21). The program provides funding to assist the states in their efforts to preserve, rehabilitate, or restore the nation's historic covered bridges. For the purposes of this program, the term "historic covered bridge" means a covered bridge that is listed or eligible for listing on the National Register for Historic Places.

For more information, write to the following address:

Federal Highway Administration
1200 New Jersey Ave. SE
Washington, DC 20590
fhwa.dot.gov

National Register of Historic Places

The National Register of Historic Places is the nation's official list of cultural resources worthy of preservation. Authorized under the National Historic Preservation Act of 1966, the National Register is part of a national program to coordinate and support public and private efforts to identify, evaluate, and protect our historic and archaeological resources.

Properties listed in the Register include districts, sites, buildings, structures, and objects that are significant in American history, architecture, archaeology, engineering, and culture. The National Park Service (NPS), which is part of the U.S. Department of the Interior, administers the National Register of Historic Places.

The official website of the National Register of Historic Places provides a searchable database of properties on the U.S. National Register, educational resources, National Historic Preservation Act requirements, preservation information resources, and virtual tours of historic sites.

For more information, write to the following address:

National Register of Historic Places
National Park Service
1201 Eye St. NW, 8th floor (MS 2280)
Washington, DC 20005
nps.gov/nr

FIRSTHAND ACCOUNTS

Gary Fischer, Architect

Gary Fischer is the principal with Arkinetics Inc., an architectural firm in Lorain, Ohio, and Cleveland, Ohio. Arkinetics is a general practice firm, handling historic preservation and adaptive reuse as well as some limited custom residential, commercial, and industrial work.

He received a B.S. and a B.Arch. from Kent State University, with an emphasis on historic preservation, renovation, and adaptive reuse. He has been working in the field since 1984 and received NCARB certification in the early 1990s.

Getting Started

"I first became interested in the field of architecture during a sixth-grade career day program. I thought it would be fun to draw buildings and to see them constructed. After graduating from college, I interviewed with several large firms (one-hundred-plus people) and several smaller ones (one or two people). I was offered a job with a large firm that designed mostly malls and retail stores. I knew that the pay would be more than adequate, but I thought that the work would be boring, so I decided against taking the job. I went back to a small firm that did more creative work and convinced them to hire me.

"I served my three-year apprenticeship working there and helped the owner increase the size of the firm to seven people. During that time, I was studying for my five-day licensing test so I would become a registered architect. One afternoon, the owner announced that he would never make another architect a partner. Since I had a limited future at that company, I planned starting up my own firm with two other employees who felt the same way I did. We discussed leaving with our boss and assured him we would not steal his clients and would be willing to assist him in easing the transition caused by our departure. We staggered our departure dates so he could bring in new employees.

"After almost a year of planning our company, Arkinetics, was born. Our first project was a building renovation."

What the Work Is Like

"Today, my job is to act as a principal of Arkinetics. It is not the least bit boring. I start a typical week by making out the work assignment schedule for the draftspeople. In this meeting, we discuss the status of each project and its expected completion date. After that I might leave the office to meet with the contractor(s) on a construction site and observe their work. Later, I might tour an existing office, store, or factory to prepare a proposal for a client needing more space or a renovation. I frequently interview people to discuss their needs for a project. I prepare design sketches and color drawings for clients to review and make presentations to clients, city governments, planning boards, and civic groups.

"In general, architects work between forty and sixty hours per week. The job can be stressful at times because of tight project schedules or difficulties during the construction process.

"Our projects range from re-creating an authentic barn with modern conveniences (hidden of course) to be used as a park visitor center in a historic park, to high-tech corporate offices and industrial buildings for a variety of companies. Visiting the facilities is one of the most interesting parts of my job. I have watched automotive parts being assembled and seen injection molders creating parts for a costume in a Disney movie. We have designed parks along the shores of Lake Erie, renovated two historic buildings to be used as home recording studios, designed loft-style apartments in old commercial buildings, and helped to create a new community for 450 new homes and shops in the heart of a depressed community. On one occasion, I was interviewed for a PBS video about the construction of a local historic monument.

"Because we are under such pressure to meet deadlines, I like to keep the office atmosphere friendly and light. We all pitch in like a team to accomplish our work. It's stressful but fun. The least enjoyable parts of my job are the evening board meetings and the tight time schedules."

Salaries

"Principals' and most architects' salaries are based on skills: better skills, better pay."

Advice from Gary Fischer

"To be a successful architect, you should possess dedication, good verbal and written communication skills, imagination, and a love of creativity. Be prepared for five grueling years of college. As you watch your friends go home for the weekend or out with friends, you will be completing a project for a class deadline. At those times, the decision you make will determine whether you have the dedication to become an architect.

"Math, physics, and art courses in high school will help in the college years. And remember to draw and sketch as much as possible. I started with a class of about 190 students in my freshman year at Kent. Forty students graduated after five years. Several went on to easier fields at the urging of the professors; they became doctors."

Peter Benton, Architect

Peter Benton is a restoration architect, specializing in historic preservation. He earned a B.S. in architecture, in 1972, from the University of Virginia in Charlottesville. He worked for several years for various firms in Philadelphia and Washington, D.C., and completed his M.Arch. from the University of Pennsylvania in 1979.

Getting Started

"Initially, I had relatively little training in preservation, but I was exposed to the idea of ecological planning at UPenn. I saw the philosophical connection between an ecological approach to the landscape and the buildings, and that led me to historic preservation. I went to work for four or five years for an ecological planning firm, where my interest developed further.

"I am now a senior associate with John Milner and Associates, Inc., a midsize architectural firm in West Chester, Pennsylvania, specializing in historic preservation. I joined the staff in 1984 and have worked on many projects."

What the Work Is Like

"I've been responsible for all sorts of properties: anything from small, privately owned residential-scale houses from the eighteenth century to high-style nineteenth-century mansions. In addition, I've worked with historic commercial and industrial buildings from the nineteenth century, restoring them or practicing what we call adaptive reuse. For example, we recently converted an old mill into an office building and a farmhouse into a meeting facility.

"Another category I've worked with includes monumental buildings, such as a city hall, or large federal buildings.

"First, I meet with the client and determine the goals for the property. Then I do an existing conditions analysis of the site, look at the historical development of the building over time, and take photographs, field measurements, and written notes.

"Next, I do a schematic plan, making preliminary drawings and sketches, describing a design for the client's approval. This stage could take four weeks or so. Once the client approves the project, I produce an outline of the scope of work and figure an order-of-magnitude cost estimate.

"After that stage is approved, the next phase is to work on design development documents. This involves the use of more detailed drawings and can take from six to eight weeks. Over the next eight to twelve weeks, construction documents including drawings and specifications are produced. During the bidding phase, the contractor is selected. If necessary, we review and revise the construction plans before beginning work. I make frequent visits to the site while the project is progressing.

"Construction time varies but could take eight months to a year and a half depending upon the scope of the project."

Salaries

"Salaries depend on the size of the firm, the importance of the project, and the region of the country. Advancement would depend on your ability and accomplishments. Those with specializations in demand can earn more."

Advice from Peter Benton

"Most firms offer paid internships for graduate students, and it is a good idea to set one up for yourself. It gives you a foot in the door when it comes time to make arrangements for a full-time job when you graduate."

TEACHING ARCHITECTURE

The discipline of architecture is rooted in an understanding of the history of the field, its role in cultural development, and the ideas that shape architects and architecture. Some architects choose the pursuit of these roots as their life's work. This decision almost always requires advanced education, increasingly at the doctoral level, and leads to teaching and research appointments in architecture schools, art and cultural history departments, or museums and academies dedicated to the development of the field.

As we learned in Chapter 2, 107 schools in the United States and 10 in Canada offer professional programs in architecture leading to the Bachelor of Architecture or Master of Architecture degree (see Appendix C). According to the National Architectural Accrediting Board (NAAB), 12,221 students were enrolled in full-time B.Arch. accredited programs and 1,127 were enrolled as part-time students in the United States in 2006. Full-time M.Arch. candidates totaled 5,664, and there were 656 part-time master's-level students.

All those students need teachers. According to the National Architectural Accrediting Board, currently there are 1,456 full-time faculty and 2,162 part-time in the United States. To give you an idea of the scope of architecture education, here is a breakdown of those numbers, prepared by the NAAB.

Full-Time Faculty Totals	1,456
Women	359
African-American	69
Native American	8
Asian/Pacific Isle	81
Hispanic	108

Part-Time Faculty Totals	2,162
Women	458
African-American	58
Native American	1
Asian/Pacific Isle	91
Hispanic	117

Total Tenured Faculty	834
Women	157
African-American	37
Native American	2
Asian/Pacific Isle	33
Hispanic	51

JOB OUTLOOK FOR ARCHITECTURE FACULTY

Between 2000 and 2020, the traditional college-age population (eighteen to twenty-four years of age) will grow somewhat slowly. This population increase, along with a higher proportion of eighteen- to twenty-four-year-olds attending college and a growing number of part-time, female, minority, and older students, will spur college enrollments. Enrollment is projected to rise from 17.5 million in 2005 to 20.4 million in 2016, an increase of about 16 percent.

More students will necessitate hiring more faculty members to teach them. At the same time, many faculty members will be retiring, opening up additional positions. The number of doctoral degrees is expected to grow slowly through 2012, somewhat easing the competition for some faculty positions.

Despite expected job growth and the need to replace retiring faculty, many in the academic community are concerned that institutions will increasingly favor the hiring of adjunct faculty over full-time, tenure-track faculty. Tenure-track positions are expected to continue declining through 2016. For many years, keen competition for faculty jobs forced some applicants to accept part-time academic appointments that offered little hope of tenure and forced others to seek nonacademic positions.

Many colleges, faced with reduced state funding for higher education and growing numbers of part-time and older students, increased the hiring of part-time faculty to save money on pay and benefits and to accommodate the needs of nontraditional-age students. In 2006, thirty percent of college faculty worked part time. If funding remains tight over the projection period, this trend of hiring adjunct or part-time faculty is likely to continue. Because of uncertainty about future funding sources, some colleges and universities are controlling costs by changing the mix of academic programs offered, eliminating some programs, adding Internet-based distance learning programs, and increasing class size. Even if the proportion of full-time positions does not shrink, job competition will remain keen for coveted tenure-track jobs. Some institutions are expected to hire more full-time faculty on limited-term contracts, reducing the number of tenure-track positions available.

Overall, postsecondary teaching positions are projected to grow faster than average through 2016. However, job prospects will continue to be better in certain fields (for example, business, architecture, engineering, health science, and computer science) that offer attractive nonacademic job opportunities and attract fewer applicants for academic positions. Excellent job prospects in vocational fields, for example, construction trades, result in higher student enrollments and increase faculty needs in that field. When more architects are needed, more architectural instructors are needed.

WHO TEACHES ARCHITECTURE

That old saying, "those who can, do; those who can't, teach," couldn't be further from the truth when it comes to architecture. Many faculty members start out as practicing architects and leave the field full-time to teach or to supplement their work with part-time teaching. (Conversely, some part-time faculty members who have not yet landed full-time, tenure-track positions do design or other related work to supplement their income.) Still others have retired from full-time architecture work and act as consultants or become faculty members. For the most part, all university faculty members in architecture must have had real-time field experience before they can find employment teaching students.

FACULTY RESPONSIBILITIES

According to a 2006 study conducted by the NAAB, full-time faculty average 13.92 student contact hours per week, and those working part-time average 7.46 contact hours. In addition to class time and student consultation, faculty members may serve on academic or administrative committees that deal with the policies of their institution, departmental matters, academic issues, curricula, budgets, equipment purchases, and hiring. Some work with student and community organizations outside the classroom.

Every college and university faculty must have a head of each concentration offered at the school. These important people oversee the curriculum and courses offered in their area, which includes the faculty members, and they report to the dean of the college or university. These people are called department chairpersons, and they are faculty members who may teach some courses but usually have heavier administrative and managerial responsibilities.

The proportion of time spent on research, teaching, administrative, and other duties varies by individual circumstance and type of institution. Faculty members at universities normally spend a significant part of their time doing research. Those in four-year colleges spend less time; and those in two-year colleges spend relatively little time. The teaching load, however, can be heavier in two-year colleges and somewhat lower at four-year institutions. Full professors at all types of institutions usually spend more time conducting research than do assistant professors, instructors, and lecturers.

Faculty members may instruct undergraduate or graduate students or both. They may give lectures to several hundred students in large halls, lead small seminars, or supervise students in design studios. They prepare lectures, exercises, and assignments; they grade exams and papers; and they advise and work with students individually. In universities, they supervise graduate students' teaching and research. College faculty members work with an increasingly varied student population made up of growing shares of part-time, older, and culturally and racially diverse students.

Faculty keep abreast of developments in their field by reading current literature, talking with colleagues, and participating in professional conferences. They may conduct their own research to expand knowledge in their field.

SALARIES FOR ARCHITECTURE FACULTY

Most college and university faculty members can be categorized into four academic ranks: professor, associate professor, assistant professor, and instructor. These positions are usually considered to be tenure-track positions. A small number of faculty members, called lecturers, are not usually on the tenure track.

According to the 2006 NAAB study, architecture faculty members have the following average annual earnings:

Professors	
National average	$69,172
Public institution	$81,939
Private institution	$59,810
Associate Professors	
National average	$52,704
Public institution	$61,981
Private institution	$45,900
Assistant Professors	
National average	$45,075
Public institution	$52,789
Private institution	$39,412

Earnings vary according to faculty rank and type of institution, geographic area, and field. According to a 2006–2007 survey by the American Association of University Professors (AAUP), salaries for full-time faculty (except those in two-year colleges that have no faculty ranks) across all fields averaged $73,207. By rank, the average was the following:

Professors	$98,974
Associate professors	$69,911
Assistant professors	$58,662
Instructors	$42,609
Lecturers	$48,289

Faculty in four-year institutions earn higher salaries, on the average, than those in two-year schools. Average salaries for faculty in public institutions ($71,362) were lower in 2006–2007 than those for private independent institutions ($84,249) but were higher than those for religiously affiliated private colleges and universities ($66,118). In fields with high-paying nonacademic alternatives (notably, medicine, law, engineering, and business), earnings exceeded these averages. In others, such as the humanities and education, they were lower.

Most faculty members have significant earnings in addition to their base salary, from consulting, teaching additional courses, researching, writing for publication, or other employment. In addition, most enjoy some unique benefits, including access to campus facilities, tuition waivers for dependents, housing and travel allowances, and paid sabbatical leaves. Conversely, part-time faculty usually have fewer benefits than full-time faculty. This can mean little or no health insurance, retirement benefits, and sabbatical leave. Because of this, some colleges and universities may attempt to cut costs by employing more part-time faculty members than full-time.

TRAINING FOR UNIVERSITY FACULTY

Four-year colleges and universities generally hire doctoral degree holders for full-time, tenure-track positions but may hire master's degree holders or doctoral candidates for certain disciplines or for part-time and temporary jobs.

Doctoral programs usually take four to seven years of full-time study beyond the bachelor's degree. Programs include increasingly specialized courses and seminars plus comprehensive examinations on all major areas of the field. They include a dissertation, which is a report on original research to answer some significant question in the field.

FINDING THAT JOB

Special publications on higher education, available in libraries and online, such as the *Chronicle of Higher Education*, list specific employment opportunities for faculty. Contact the specific institution in which you are interested to learn about openings, but be prepared to relocate. With only 129 accredited institutions in Canada and the United States, you will probably have to move to find work.

SAMPLE JOB LISTINGS

These listings are provided as a sample only, and as such, the hiring firms are not mentioned. You may find similar job listings by visiting websites for the Chronicle of Higher Education (chronicle.com) and related professional associations or by performing an Internet search using keywords such as university, teaching, jobs, and architecture.

Assistant Professor—School of Landscape Architecture Education

Requirements: Applicants must hold an advanced degree. At least one degree must be from an accredited program in landscape architecture. The Ph.D. degree, or an interdisciplinary degree, is highly desirable. Fluency in a foreign language is beneficial. Professional registration, though not required, is advantageous.

The School of Landscape Architecture invites applications for a tenure-track, academic-year appointment at the Assistant Professor level. The successful applicant will teach courses in Landscape Planning and Geographic Information Systems, as well as other areas within the professional curriculum. The School of Landscape Architecture is one of three units in the College of Architecture, Planning, and Landscape Architecture (CAPLA). The graduate professional program offers the Master of Landscape Architecture degree as an accredited, three-year curriculum. Current enrollment is approximately fifty graduate students.

Assistant Professor—Department of Architecture
Minimum qualification: Master of Architecture degree or master's degree in a related field with curriculum equivalency.

Preferred qualifications: registration (license to practice architecture); quality of design work and/or evidence of contributions to the profession through practice and service; record of previous teaching experience and commitment to work in a collaborative environment; and publications and/or appropriate research work as evidence of scholarly contributions.

Responsibilities: teaching design studios and courses in computer design and providing leadership in the development of the curriculum in the area of computational tools for designing.

Architecture/Urban Planning
Requirements: Applicants must have a professional degree and a master's degree in an appropriate specialty with a minimum of three years' experience in professional practice and/or teaching experience at the undergraduate level. Preference will be given to applicants with a Ph.D. degree or equivalent. Applicants in Urban Planning must have a Ph.D. Applicants must be able to show evidence of quality design production and an active and ongoing research agenda.

The Department of Architecture and Design has openings in Architecture and Urban Planning for the upcoming academic year, including continuing appointments and visiting positions for two semesters' duration. Salary and rank are commensurate with qualifications.

FIRSTHAND ACCOUNT

John Downs, Professor

John Downs is a full professor at a prestigious architecture institution in New York City. The courses he has taught over the years include basic and advanced design courses, architectural materials, structure, architectural history, cultural history, planning, construction documentation, and a range of electives. He earned his B.Arch. in 1967 and his Ph.D. in 1977.

Getting Started

"A bachelor's in architecture is not necessary to go on for further study at the doctorate level. I was interested in doing research that was more humanistic than applied.

"A fellow student who had a job told me of their search for a new faculty member. I was not satisfied with the working conditions where I was. I was still writing my Ph.D. dissertation and felt this new university would be a hospitable place to finish it. I was supporting a wife and child at the time and needed a job that would provide income as well as a relaxed atmosphere in which I could finish writing my field research. The university where I was working before had no interest in advancing the instructors and put a heavy teaching load on them."

What the Work Is Like

"A university job in architecture is much like a job with a professional program in any other field. The job depends more on the institution for which you work than on the discipline in which you teach.

"The most coveted jobs at universities are the ones that lead to tenure. Tenure guarantees that the person will not be fired for teaching what he or she feels is right; however the person has to prove the quality of his or her teaching and scholarship before being granted tenure. This usually takes five or more years.

"Before getting tenure, a faculty member usually has to work hard proving that he or she can produce scholarship of a quality that gets his or her work published in good journals. Innovative and creative ideas are often appreciated by one's peers, but they may not be recognized in the tenure-granting process. Quality teaching is important.

"Before and after tenure, university faculty people work hard. They are usually dedicated to their job. They may concentrate on doing new research, setting up academic programs, supervising student research, or teaching. There is a great opportunity to know students and help them mature personally and professionally. Many faculty members find great rewards in this.

"I usually spend ten or twelve hours a day doing something related to my job. I work as much as I can without jeopardizing my family life or friendships. This means that I usually work at something in the evening or on the weekends. It is often hard to define the boundary between work and leisure.

"The least pleasant part of my work is the bureaucratic requirements of my job. These do not bother everyone, and many faculty members enjoy participating in the bureaucratic structure of the university. The pleasantness of the bureaucracy can vary from university to university. Fortunately, I do not work for a university in which strong management has the upper hand and treats the faculty like stupid employees. It may sound ridiculous, but there is a tendency in American universities for 'professional,' rather academically untrained administrations to develop. They pay less attention to the academic values of the university, and life can be made miserable for everyone. Work for a university in which academic values, which include positive experiences for students, are put first.

"I don't like to give exams and hand out grades. I would like all my students to be fascinated by the subject matter and do the best they can, but alas, they have varied goals and interests. Human nature places limits on the freedom that one can give to students, and therefore the structure of teaching can be a burden at times."

Advice from John Downs

"Check to see what the unemployment level is for the degree you are pursuing. Architecture could have a rather high level of Ph.D. unemployment. Be honest in examining your motives. Ask yourself if you are willing to put up with long years of graduate education, long years of field work, and long years of job hunting, and you may have to move in order to secure a desirable position."

PART TWO

Related Fields

CHAPTER 6

LANDSCAPE ARCHITECTURE

Everyone enjoys attractive residential areas, public parks, college campuses, shopping centers, parkways, golf courses, and industrial parks. Landscape architects design these areas so they are functional, beautiful, and compatible with the natural environment. They may plan the location of buildings, roads, and walkways and the arrangement of flowers, shrubs, and trees. Historic preservation and natural resource conservation and reclamation are other important objectives to which landscape architects may apply their knowledge of the environment, design, and artistic talents.

Landscape architects are hired by many types of organizations, such as real estate development firms starting new projects and municipalities constructing airports or parks. They can be involved with the development of a site from its conception. Working with architects, engineers, scientists, and other professionals, they help determine the best arrangement of roads and buildings to conserve or restore natural resources. Once these decisions are made, landscape architects create detailed plans indicating new topography, vegetation, walkways, and landscape amenities.

In planning a site, landscape architects first consider the project's nature and purpose and the available funds. They analyze the site's natural elements, such as the climate, soil, slope of the land, drainage, and vegetation. They observe where sunlight falls on the site at different times of the day and examine the site from various angles. They assess the effect of existing buildings, roads, walkways, and utilities.

After studying and analyzing the site, landscape architects prepare a preliminary design. To account for the client's needs as well as the site conditions, they may have to make many changes before a final design is approved. They must account for any local, state, or federal regulations, such as those protecting wetlands or historic resources.

An increasing number of landscape architects are using computer-aided design (CAD) systems to assist them in preparing their designs. Many landscape architects use video simulation as a tool to help clients envision the proposed ideas and plans. For larger-scale site planning, landscape architects use geographic information systems (GIS) technology, which is a computer mapping system.

Throughout all phases of the planning and design, landscape architects consult with other professionals involved in the project. Once the design is complete, they prepare a proposal for the client. They produce detailed site plans, including written reports, sketches, models, photographs, land-use studies, and cost estimates, and submit them for approval by the client and by regulatory agencies. If the plans are approved, landscape architects prepare working drawings showing all existing and proposed features. They outline in detail the construction methods and create a list of necessary materials. Even though many landscape architects supervise the installation of their design, some are involved in the site construction. In general, however, this work is done by the developer or landscape contractor.

Some landscape architects work on many projects. Others specialize in a particular area, such as residential development, historic landscape restoration, waterfront improvement projects, parks and playgrounds, or shopping centers. Still others work in regional planning and resource management; feasibility, environmental impact, and cost studies; or site construction. Some landscape architects teach in colleges or universities.

Even though most landscape architects do at least some residential work, few limit their practice to landscape design for individual homeowners. This is because most residential landscape design projects are too small to provide suitable income compared with larger commercial or multiunit residential projects. For these kinds of smaller projects, some nurseries offer residential landscape design services. However, less qualified landscape designers or others with training and experience in related areas can perform these services.

Landscape architects who work for government agencies do similar work at national parks, government buildings, and other government-owned facilities. In addition, they may prepare environmental impact statements (EIS) and studies on environmental issues such as public land-use planning. All landscape architects combine their knowledge of design, construction, plants, soils, and ecology to create their final designs.

WORKING CONDITIONS

Landscape architects spend most of their time in offices creating plans and designs, preparing models and cost estimates, doing research, or attending meetings. The remainder of their time is spent at the site. During the design and planning stage, landscape architects visit and analyze the site to verify that the design can be incorporated into the landscape. After the plans and specifications are completed, they may spend additional time at the site observing or supervising the construction. Those who work in large firms may spend considerably more time out of the office because of travel to sites outside the local area. Salaried employees in government and landscape architectural firms usually work regular hours, though they may work overtime to meet a project deadline; the hours of self-employed landscape architects may vary from project to project.

EMPLOYMENT FIGURES

In 2006, landscape architects held more than 28,000 jobs nationwide. More than one out of two landscape architects were employed in architectural and engineering firms, with landscaping service firms employing about 17 percent of the rest. The federal government employs these workers, primarily in the U.S. Departments of Agriculture, Defense, and the Interior. About two of every five landscape architects are self-employed. Most landscape architects find work in urban and suburban areas throughout the country, though some landscape architects work in rural areas, particularly those in the federal government who plan and design parks and recreation areas.

JOB OUTLOOK

According to the U.S. Bureau of Labor Statistics (BLS), employment of landscape architects is expected to increase faster than average for all occupations through the year 2016. The level of new construction plays an important role in determining demand for landscape architects. Increased development of open space into recreation areas, wildlife refuges, and parks will require the skills of landscape architects. Overall, anticipated growth in construction is expected to increase demand for landscape architectural services.

The recent passage of the Transportation Equity Act for the 21st Century (TEA-21) is expected to spur employment for landscape architects, particularly in state and local governments. TEA-21 provides funds for surface transportation and transit programs, such as interstate highway maintenance and environmentally friendly pedestrian and bicycle trails. However, opportunities will vary from year to year and by geographic region, depending on local economic conditions. During a recession, when real estate sales and construction decelerate, landscape architects may face layoffs and greater job competition. The need to replace landscape architects who retire or leave the labor force for other reasons is expected to produce as many job openings as employment growth.

An increasing proportion of office and other commercial and industrial development will occur outside cities. These projects are typically located on larger sites with more surrounding land that needs to be designed by a landscape architect, in contrast to urban development, which often includes little or no surrounding land.

As the cost of land rises, the importance of good site planning and landscape design will grow. Increasingly, new development is contingent upon compliance with environmental regulations and land-use zoning, spurring demand for landscape architects to help plan sites and integrate man-made structures with the natural environment in the least disruptive way.

Budget tightening in the federal government might restrict hiring in the USDA Forest Service and the National Park Service (NPS), agencies that traditionally employ the most landscape architects in the federal government. Instead, such agencies may increasingly contract out for landscape architecture services, providing additional employment opportunities in private landscape architecture firms.

In addition to the work related to new development and construction, landscape architects are expected to be involved in historic preservation, land reclamation, and refurbishment of existing sites. Because landscape architects can work on many different types of projects, they may have an easier time than other design professionals finding employment when traditional construction decelerates.

New graduates can expect competition for jobs in the largest and most prestigious landscape architecture firms. The number of professional degrees awarded in landscape architecture has remained steady even during times of fluctuating demand due to economic conditions. Opportunities will be best for landscape architects who develop strong technical and communication skills and a knowledge of environmental codes and regulations. Those with additional training or experience in urban planning increase their opportunities for employment in landscape architecture firms that specialize in site planning as well as landscape design. Many employers prefer to hire entry-level landscape architects who have internship experience, which reduces the amount of on-the-job training required.

TRAINING FOR LANDSCAPE ARCHITECTS

A bachelor's or master's degree in landscape architecture is usually necessary for entry into the profession. The bachelor's degree in landscape architecture takes four or five years to complete.

There are two types of accredited master's degree programs. The master's degree as a first professional degree is a three-year program designed for students with an undergraduate degree in another discipline. This is the most common type. The master's degree as the second professional degree is a two-year program for students who have a bachelor's degree in landscape architecture and wish to teach or specialize in some aspect of landscape architecture, such as regional planning or golf course design.

In 2007, sixty-one colleges and universities offered seventy-nine undergraduate and graduate programs in landscape architecture, accredited by the Landscape Architecture Accreditation Board (LAAB) of the American Society of Landscape Architects (ASLA).

College courses required in this field usually include technical subjects, such as surveying, landscape design and construction, landscape ecology, site design, and urban and regional planning. Other courses include history of landscape architecture, plant and soil science, geology, professional practice, and general management.

Many landscape architecture programs are adding courses that address environmental issues. Most students at the undergraduate level take a year of prerequisite courses such as English, mathematics, and social and physical science. The design studio is an important aspect of many landscape architecture curriculums. Whenever possible, students are assigned real projects, providing them with valuable hands-on experience. While working on these projects, students become more proficient in CAD, GIS, and video simulation.

In 2008, forty-nine states required landscape architects to be licensed or registered. Licensing is based on the Landscape Architect Registration Examination (LARE), sponsored by the Council of Landscape Architectural Registration Boards (CLARB) and administered over a three-day period. Exam admission usually requires a degree from an accredited school plus one to four years of work experience, though standards vary from state to state.

Currently, fifteen states require the passage of a state examination in addition to the LARE to satisfy registration requirements. State examinations, which are usually one hour and completed at the end of the LARE, focus on laws, environmental regulations, plants, soils, climate, and any other characteristics unique to the state.

Because state requirements for licensure are not uniform, landscape architects may not find it easy to transfer their registration from one state to another. However, those who meet the national standards of graduating from an accredited program, serving three years of internship under the supervision of a registered landscape architect, and passing the LARE can satisfy most states' requirements. Through these means, a landscape architect can obtain CLARB certification and gain reciprocity in other states.

In the federal government, candidates for entry positions should have a bachelor's or master's degree in landscape architecture. Unlike state requirements, the federal government does not require its landscape architects to be licensed.

SKILLS NEEDED FOR LANDSCAPE ARCHITECTURE

People planning a career in landscape architecture should appreciate nature, enjoy working with their hands, and possess strong analytical skills. Creative vision and artistic talent are desirable qualities. Good oral communication skills are essential since landscape architects must be able to convey their ideas to other professionals and clients and to make presentations before large groups. Strong writing skills are valuable, as is the knowledge of computer applications, including word processing, desktop publishing, and spreadsheets. Landscape architects will use all these tools to develop presentations, proposals, reports, and land impact studies for clients, colleagues, and superiors. The ability to draft and design using CAD is essential. Many employers recommend that prospective landscape architects complete at least one summer internship with a landscape architecture firm to gain an understanding of the daily operations of a small business, including how to win clients, generate fees, and work within a budget. In addition, a landscape architect may have to do the following on a daily basis:

- Attend to client needs; take responsibility for timely, effective responses
- Be multitask oriented; can coordinate various projects at one time
- Be willing and capable of participating in making public presentations
- Have an understanding of municipal entitlement processes
- Have good verbal, written, and graphic communication skills
- Have a working knowledge of AutoCAD 2000, MS Word, and Excel

INTERN LANDSCAPE ARCHITECTS

In states where licensure is required, new hires may be called apprentices or intern landscape architects until they become licensed. Their duties vary depending on the firm's type and size. They may do project research or prepare working drawings, construction documents, or base maps of the area to be landscaped. Some are allowed to participate in the actual project design. However, interns must perform all work under the supervision of a licensed landscape architect.

Additionally, all drawings and specifications must be signed and sealed by the licensed landscape architect, who takes legal responsibility for the work. After gaining experience and becoming licensed, landscape architects usually can carry a design through all the development stages. After several years, they may become project managers, taking on the responsibility for meeting schedules and budgets and for overseeing the project design, and later they may become associates or partners, with a proprietary interest in the business.

SELF-EMPLOYMENT

Many landscape architects are self-employed because start-up costs, after an initial investment in CAD software, can be low. Self-discipline, business acumen, and good marketing skills are important qualities for those who choose to open their own business. Even with these qualities, however, some architects may struggle while building a client base and reputation in the community.

RELATED FIELDS

Those with landscape architecture training qualify for jobs closely related to landscape architecture and may, after gaining some experience, become construction supervisors, land or environmental planners, or landscape consultants. Landscape architects use their knowledge of design, construction, land-use planning, and environmental issues to develop a landscape project. Others whose work requires similar skills are architects, surveyors, civil engineers, soil conservationists, and urban and regional planners. Landscape architects know how to grow and use plants in the landscape. Botanists, who study plants in general, and horticulturists, who study ornamental plants as well as fruit, vegetable, greenhouse, and nursery crops, do similar work.

Landscape Design

A landscape designer's work is similar to that of a landscape architect, usually on residential or small commercial projects. Landscape designers are not technically certified; therefore, they cannot call themselves landscape architects. For those who do not wish to invest the time to become a landscape architect, a career in landscape design could be the answer. You can become a landscape designer after completing a two-year associate's degree in a landscape specialist program offered at a number of U.S. schools. Salaries are generally less for designers than for architects. On the upside, those who are self-employed are not as limited as those employed by a landscape architecture firm.

Work in landscape design is available almost anywhere you see a tree, shrub, or lawn. Job seekers do not have to scour help wanted ads or move across the country to find employment, though doing so could help broaden the scope. Just look around you at all the possibilities. Each of the following settings requires a range of workers:

Arboretums	Historic areas	Private homes
Athletic fields	Hospitals	Public parks and gardens
Botanical gardens	Hotels	Recreational facilities
Cemeteries	Museums	Shopping malls
Golf courses	Office buildings	Theme parks
Highways	Playgrounds	University campuses

Historic Landscape Preservation and Landscape Archaeology

Historic landscape preservation is a field of growing interest throughout the country among managers of historic buildings and cultural and natural landscapes. The Colonial Williamsburg Foundation in Williamsburg, Virginia, is one of the largest employers of landscape architects, designers, and related groundskeeping professionals.

Landscape archeology is a fairly new discipline, with the purpose of recovering enough evidence to re-create a garden that existed on the site in a given historical period. Landscape archaeology uses traditional archaeological techniques to recover the fence lines, planting beds, and other evidence.

Just as with gardening history, there is no particular university degree at this time in landscape archaeology. To become a landscape archaeologist, follow a traditional program in anthropology and archaeology. Once you have graduated and started getting on-the-job experience, you could specialize. (For more information on historic landscape preservation and landscape archaeology, see Kent Brinkley's firsthand account later in this chapter.)

Interiorscaping

An interiorscaper works with clients who want to create indoor environments filled with plants. The interiorscaper provides the design, oversees the installation, and if the contract specifies, maintains the health and attractiveness of the layout. Interiorscapers find work with large landscape contracting firms or nurseries, or they can go independent, renting space with adequate lighting in a warehouse where they can store their plants. Some large land developers, rather than contracting the work out, hire permanent on-staff interiorscapers to take care of the malls or other complexes they own. Even though private homeowners might utilize an interiorscaper's services, most clients come from the commercial world.

Within the field of interiorscaping are several different job titles, including designers, estimators, and operations managers. Interiorscapers utilize the services of installers, delivery people, and job installation supervisors. Maintenance technicians take care of the plants, and maintenance foremen supervise the technicians. Nurseries that employ interiorscapers hire competent sales staff to interact with customers.

The chance for advancement is good within the industry. With some experience under their belts, installers and maintenance technicians, for example, can move to supervisory or sales positions. Many people start out established in the floral business, as florists or floral designers, for example, and interiorscaping becomes a natural extension of what they are doing. A flower shop owner, for example, might stock tropical houseplants for retail. Through walk-in customers from local office buildings, the florist could be requested to add installation and maintenance services.

Entry-level crew workers and technicians can start anywhere from $6 to $14 an hour, with a median of $10.27 an hour for landscaping and groundskeepers in 2006. Someone with a new bachelor's degree could expect to earn in the teens or twenties, depending on the country region. Designers and managers' average annual earnings vary from $48,000 to $82,760 per year.

JOB HUNTING

With the Internet, job hunting has become easier. You are no longer restricted to your own hometown paper or trekking to the library to dig out the yellow pages for other regions. A search on the Web will produce dozens, maybe hundreds, of hits. A visit to the official website of the American Society of Landscape Architects (asla.org) will bring you to a database of job listings.

SAMPLE JOB LISTINGS

These listings are provided as a sample only; therefore, the hiring firms are not mentioned. You may find similar listings by visiting the ASLA website.

Entry-Level Landscape Architect, Arizona

A small, well-established landscape architecture firm is looking for someone with the qualities of a self-starter (motivated, goal-oriented, responsible) who is a quick learner. The ability to work well alone and with a team is a must. The right individual will be proficient in AutoCAD (we have Release 14) and will have the drafting abilities required for occasional hand-drawn items. Knowledge of Southwestern plants and quick, high-quality rendering abilities are a plus. We provide a casual business atmosphere. A full benefits package is offered, with available flex hour options. Our projects cover a wide range, but most are commercial and multifamily projects.

Experience required: none to two years.

Education requirements: B.L.A. or equivalent from an accredited university.

Landscape Architect, Louisiana

We are in search of a motivated self-starter, excited about learning and working the craft of landscape architecture. Our projects vary in scope, scale, and clientele. All are site/construction oriented and premised on advancing technical expertise, design excellence, and construction craftsmanship. This is a small, custom-design studio and not a production sweatshop. Our studio extends to the construction site. We like muddy boots, plants, current technology, and old-fashioned nuts-and-bolts know-how. If you're looking for a traditional, craft-based landscape architecture opportunity and can demonstrate excellent examples of your own dedication and focus, please contact us for a meeting.

Experience required: one to three years.

Education requirements: landscape architect: B.L.A./M.L.A., or others with appropriate supporting skills; horticultural knowledge; strong design skills; construction experience; AutoCAD 14/2000 design and production skills; project management; a rounded perspective on life.

Landscape Architect Assistant, Louisiana

We are in need of an ambitious, mature, design-oriented self-starter who is working toward becoming a career professional. Duties involve participation in all aspects of project management, design, and CAD-based drafting production, office operations, and limited field-related activities. This is a wide-open opportunity to learn by doing, assist project designers, meet clients, work in a small, creative studio environment, and participate in on-site design and construction-phase activities. This position demands self-discipline, motivation, and teamwork. In addition to professional-related activities, general office assistance regarding daily business operations is included. All work will be preformed under the immediate supervision of a registered landscape architect.

Experience required: none.

Education requirements: bachelor's degree; award from recognized certificate program in landscape architecture, architecture, or complimentary discipline; and AutoCAD and other computer experience preferred.

Green Space Design, Utah

Green Space Design is a new idea and landscape architecture realm developed by an award-winning firm focused on preserving landscapes. Green Space Design designs open space into community plans, connecting critical lands into one system. The process defines open space types, utilizes GIS and satellite imagery to map them, calls on public participation to identify and design a green space vision, and implements that vision through a spectrum of planning and preservation tools. A green space is created commensurate with growth, building a green infrastructure that balances preservation and development economically and equitably.

This is a project manager position within a three-person core of land designers, involving interviews/meetings/presentations with community members; landscape analysis/mapping; and updating planning documents. Essential abilities include superior written, verbal, and graphic communication; a commitment to marketing projects; moderate computer skills (desktop publishing, GIS, CAD); a comprehensive understanding of land and natural systems; and ability to travel the Intermountain Region. The ideal candidate should be versed and vocal in land conservation, smart growth, and public participation in planning.

Experience required: three years desired, but enthusiasm and interest weigh heavily.

Education requirements: B.L.A. or M.L.A.

Landscape Architect Extraordinaire, Vermont

A firm of three-hundred-plus planners, engineers, landscape architects, and scientists is looking for a landscape architect (guru) to lead and manage its Landscape Architecture and Planning Group. You will be working with a staff of talented and motivated landscape architects and planners, coordinating with our fifteen offices in the Northeast, Southeast, and Southwest. You must be an innovator, mentor, doer-seller, with a whatever-it-takes attitude. If you are ready to live in a gorgeous place, work hard for a company that offers great pay and benefits, and make a mark in the profession, send in your resume and portfolio.

Experience required: twenty-plus years of diverse design and leadership.

Education requirements: minimum B.L.A.

SALARIES FOR LANDSCAPE ARCHITECTS

In 2006, the median annual earnings for landscape architects was $55,140. The middle 50 percent earned between $42,270 and $73,240. The lowest 10 percent earned less than $34,230, and the highest 10 percent earned more than $95,420. Most landscape architects worked in the architecture and engineering services industry, where average (mean) annual earnings were $61,340 in 2006. In 2006, the average annual salary for all landscape architects in the federal government in nonsupervisory, supervisory, and managerial positions was about $73,210.

Because many landscape architects work for small firms or are self-employed, benefits tend to be less generous than those provided to workers in large organizations.

FIRSTHAND ACCOUNTS

Kent Brinkley, Landscape Architect

Kent Brinkley is a landscape architect and garden historian at Colonial Williamsburg Foundation. He has a B.A in history from Mary Baldwin College in Staunton, Virginia. He has been with the foundation for more than ten years.

Getting Started

"I came to landscape architecture through the back door. I started as a draftsman and worked my way up to the firm's vice president before coming to my position at the Colonial Williamsburg Foundation. When I got my job here I was ecstatic. This was the perfect marriage of my love of history and my work as a landscape architect. I have enjoyed being able to take two major interests and combine them in a way that allows me to do both."

What the Work Is Like

"I wear a lot of different hats. I sit at a drawing board and I create designs for new work that is taking place. We have many gardens designed during the 1930s and 1940s by my predecessors. They conducted extensive research and chose plants that were known and used in the eighteenth century. But in a few cases, a plant they chose, though appropriate to the period, might not be flourishing in a specific location because of too much sunlight or too much shade. So, we think of something else that would have been used but will grow better in that specific location.

"Many of these gardens are forty or fifty years old and, unlike the architecture where you just replace fabric when a board rots or you are putting a coat of paint on, plant materials do grow. They're dynamic, and when you have a garden that is mature, or overmature as many of ours happen to be, part of my charge is looking at the replacements that have to be factored in when plants or trees die out. This keeps it looking presentable to the public.

"I work closely with the person responsible for the maintenance. I provide the design expertise, and we talk about what is needed in a particular garden. Once a decision has been made, I direct my maintenance staff to implement the work.

"I spend time giving slide lectures to groups and garden clubs. I give garden tours a couple of times a month to the public to have contact with the visitors.

"I'm also a garden historian. That is someone who has a background in history and has done research and is interested in the development of the historical landscape. I've made any number of trips to England in the last fourteen or fifteen years and have visited many country estates and gardens over there. I have looked at English landscape design, which served as the precedent for many of the designs in the eighteenth century here in the Virginia Colony. Much of my work involves looking at what was done historically in gardens. The kinds of plants that were grown, how they were laid out, the types of fencing they were using is all part of knowing how to re-create a period garden.

"Someone comes to this specialty within a history curriculum. It's a young field in this country and didn't start as a discipline until 1975. If this interests you, you would combine history courses with horticulture courses. Of course, the job market is small but is growing. Most jobs are at living history museums such as Williamsburg, Sturbridge Village, and Plimoth Plantation in Massachusetts.

"Here, we have colonial gardens that have been re-created, duplicating the plants used during the eighteenth century. Beautiful three-hundred-year-old and four-hundred-year-old trees still stand, lining the hard-packed dirt walkways. All of this restoration work was accomplished after extensive archaeological and historical investigation.

"Part of my job is to work in concert with archaeologists when they are excavating a particular site. A few years ago, for example, a summer field school from the College of William and Mary was in progress. We excavated a garden in town. This particular site was the home of Saint George Tucker, a fairly prominent Virginian in the eighteenth century whose papers have survived. We know a good bit about his interest in gardening and the things he was growing, so it was exciting to see what the archaeology turned up, finding physical evidence of his garden pathways, fence lines and postholes. They leave a definite dark stain. We can find planting beds and outbuilding foundations, brick foundations of dairies and chicken coops.

"When you excavate the soil from the planting bed, you sometimes find seed materials in the soil samples. You screen the soil and take it into a lab. A method known as flotation separates the water from the soil, and any minute particles and seeds can be recovered. Using a microscope, you can identify the plant type from the seed. We can do pollen analysis, which can be problematical because you do not always know how the seeds ended up in the bed. They could have been dropped by birds or blown by wind.

"We can solve that particular problem with phytolith analysis, which examines the mineralized tissues of plants. A plant absorbs water and minerals through its root system. When a plant dies, the liquid material will crystallize; when it does, it takes on an impression of the plant cell wall structure. All the phytoliths will deposit in the soil as the plant decays. Unlike seeds or pollen, which could have gotten there for a number of reasons, when you find phytolith in the soil sample, you can be 99 percent certain the plant was grown there and didn't just happen."

Advice from Kent Brinkley

"People who are mechanically inclined or are curious how things fit together and work would probably find landscape architecture and drafting to their liking. A lot of drafting is involved, and you have to know how to cultivate that drawing talent.

"You have to have good English skills. You need the ability to write and speak well because you work with people every day. You might have to get up in front of a group and make a presentation to sell your designs. Some sales ability is a good thing to have. You have to market yourself, your firm, and the design and be able to persuade people that this is the way to go. You can never waste your time by taking additional English or drawing courses.

"Once you have graduated, you should work in different offices and gain different experiences for the first five or six years. Do not lock yourself into any one place. You should work in the field for two or three years before taking the licensing exam, which is comprehensive in scope and tests you on many things. You need to get some experience under your belt before you tackle it.

"I think there's a bright future for people in this field in the twenty-first century because we are the ones who have a broad enough range of expertise to consider environmental concerns in addition to aesthetics to make the resulting projects user-friendly and earth-friendly."

Greg Blackwell, Landscape Architect/Interiorscaper

Greg Blackwell works for Creative Plantings, a large contracting firm in Burtonsville, Maryland. He is a registered landscape architect with a strong interest in interior design. He started with a B.S. in horticulture from Virginia, specializing in landscape design.

Most interiorscaping programs fall under the auspices of a landscape architecture or landscape design program. Community colleges offer courses, but a degree is not necessary to pursue a career as an interiorscaper since many firms will take on interns and provide on-the-job training.

What the Work Is Like

"My firm works with hotels, office buildings, shopping malls, restaurants, corporate headquarters, and other types of large and small businesses. On any given project, we first meet with clients to discuss their needs, what they are looking for, from a planting and design standpoint, and their budget. In the initial visit, I get as much information as I can, including building blueprints, light readings, colors and accents in the surroundings, finishes and furniture styles, and water sources. In larger jobs, the time of year might be important. For example, because of freezing temperatures, you may have to protect material from the cold weather during the delivery process.

"Then, if possible, we like our clients to visit our facility. We have greenhouses where they can pick out particular plants. We have photographs we can show them. Depending on the person, the client might want to leave it all up to us or stay involved throughout the process.

"Next, I'll write up specifications, including detailed drawings and layout, and artist renderings, to show what the space will look like with plants and the different kinds of containers and finishes. After I work on the plans and have prepared my presentation, I meet with the clients and present my ideas. If they approve the plan, the next step is to organize and obtain the materials. If we do not have them in stock, then I will go to the growers, wholesalers, or importers in Florida, select the materials, and tag the plants I'll need.

"We schedule delivery and installation and coordinate with the other trades. Interiorscapers are usually the last people in on a project, especially with new buildings, because we have to wait until all the construction is done.

"After the job is installed, we usually come back on a weekly basis to clean the plants and inspect them for any insects or disease. If there is a situation in which sunlight is coming in strongly from one side, we will rotate the plants because they start facing toward the sun. We'll replace any plants that are doing badly.

"I am responsible for estimating, inventory, purchasing, and photography. I use photography to chronicle possible plant arrangements for customers and to enter designs into professional competitions.

"Clients of Creative Plantings have two choices: they can purchase the plants and containers outright and have a separate monthly maintenance contract, or they can lease the entire package for one monthly payment and a small up-front charge.

"We provide short-term rentals for conventions, weddings, and other types of special events, including large-scale events such as the inauguration and all the balls here in Washington, D.C."

Advice from Greg Blackwell

"I would encourage you to consider self-employment. While interiorscapers with large firms or nurseries usually have a selection of plants in stock, a self-employed designer could operate with a small inventory. Utilizing pictures, you could set up a job with a client and order the plants needed from a local wholesaler. This way, you can run a lucrative business with relatively low overhead costs."

CHAPTER 7

ENGINEERING

The design of buildings often requires the special expertise of civil, structural, architectural, mechanical, and electrical engineers. Engineers have many options and are in considerable demand from the industry and private practice, whether from corporate clients or manufacturers of building products. Engineers offering design services for building projects typically practice as independent consultants in one of the areas listed or as a specialty engineer in, for example, acoustical, illumination, or fire protection design. Some engineering firms combine two or more of these areas. For example, some may offer a combination of architecture, construction management, or design-build services.

ENGINEERING SPECIALIZATIONS

Many specialization areas exist for those interested in the engineering field, and each one is integral to the building and construction of various projects. The major specialization areas in engineering are civil, structural, architectural, and mechanical engineering, along with electrical and electronics engineering.

- **Civil engineers.** Civil engineers specialize in the design, construction, and operation of facilities essential to modern life. These include buildings, highways, airports, pipelines, bridges, dams, irrigation systems, drainage systems, water supply and distribution systems, and wastewater treatment works.

• **Structural engineers.** Structural engineers specialize in the design of bridges, buildings, telecommunications towers, dams, space platforms, amusement park rides, and more, with attention to the ability to withstand forces or loads from people, vehicles, gusting winds, extreme temperatures, earth and water pressures, earthquakes, and so on. At the undergraduate level, the study of various structural engineering topics is generally part of the course of study leading to the bachelor's degree in civil engineering.

• **Architectural engineers.** Architectural engineers specialize in the analysis, design, construction, and operation of engineered systems for commercial, industrial, and institutional buildings and other facilities. Building systems include electrical, communications and control, lighting, heating, ventilating, air-conditioning, fire protection, plumbing, acoustical, and structural systems.

• **Mechanical engineers.** Mechanical engineers specialize in the research, development, design, manufacture, and testing of tools, engines, machines, and other mechanical devices. They work on power-producing machines such as electricity-producing generators, internal combustion engines, steam and gas turbines, and jet and rocket engines. They develop power-using machines such as refrigeration and air-conditioning equipment, robots used in manufacturing, machine tools, materials handling systems, and industrial production equipment. Mechanical engineers design tools needed by other engineers for their work.

• **Electrical and electronics engineers.** Electrical and electronics engineers specialize in different areas such as power generation, transmission, and distribution; communications; computer electronics; and electrical equipment manufacturing, or a subdivision of these areas, for example, industrial robot control systems or aviation electronics. Electrical and electronics engineers design new products, write performance requirements, and develop maintenance schedules. They test equipment, solve operating problems, and estimate the time and cost of engineering projects.

POSSIBLE EMPLOYERS

Civil, structural, and architectural engineers are employed by government agencies, public utility companies, private consulting firms, construction companies, architectural firms, and universities.

Mechanical engineering is the broadest engineering discipline, extending across many interdependent specialties. Mechanical engineers work in many industries, and their work varies by industry and function.

Electrical and electronics engineering is the largest branch of engineering. Electrical and electronics engineers work for engineering and business consulting firms; government agencies; electrical and electronic equipment, industrial machinery, and professional and scientific instruments manufacturers; communications and utilities firms; manufacturers of aircraft and guided missiles; and computer and data processing services firms.

TRAINING FOR ENGINEERS

A bachelor's degree in engineering is generally required for entry-level engineering jobs. College graduates with a degree in a physical science or mathematics may qualify for some engineering jobs, especially in specialties in high demand.

Most engineering degrees are granted in electrical, mechanical, or civil engineering. However, engineers trained in one branch may work in related branches. For example, many aerospace engineers have training in mechanical engineering. This flexibility allows employers to meet staffing needs in new technologies and specialties in which engineers are in short supply. It allows engineers to shift to fields with better employment prospects or to ones that match their interests more closely.

In addition to the standard engineering degree, many colleges offer degrees in engineering technology, offered as two-year or four-year programs. These programs prepare students for practical design and production work, rather than for jobs requiring more theoretical and scientific knowledge. Graduates of four-year technology programs may get jobs similar to those obtained by graduates with a bachelor's degree in engineering. Some employers regard technology program graduates as having skills between those of a technician and an engineer.

Graduate training is essential for engineering faculty positions but is not required for most entry-level engineering jobs. Many engineers obtain graduate degrees in engineering or business administration to learn new technologies, broaden their education, and enhance their promotion opportunities. Many high-level executives in government and industry began their careers as engineers. Sometimes, architects leave the field and retrain for a career in engineering.

About 1,830 colleges and universities offer bachelor's degree programs in engineering that are accredited by the Accreditation Board for Engineering and Technology (ABET). About 710 colleges offer accredited bachelor's degree programs in engineering technology. ABET accreditation is based on an examination of an engineering program's student achievement, program improvement, faculty, curricular content, facilities, and institutional commitment. Even though most institutions offer programs in the major branches of engineering, only a few offer some of the smaller specialties. Programs of the same title may vary in content. For example, some programs emphasize industrial practices, preparing students for a job in industry, whereas others are more theoretical and are better for students preparing to take on graduate work. Therefore, students should investigate curricula and check accreditation carefully before selecting a college.

Admissions requirements for undergraduate engineering schools include a solid background in mathematics (algebra, geometry, trigonometry, and calculus), sciences (biology, chemistry, and physics), and courses in English, social studies, humanities, and computers.

Bachelor's degree programs in engineering are typically designed to last four years, but many students find that it takes between four and five years to complete their studies. In a typical four-year college curriculum, the first two years are spent studying mathematics, basic sciences, introductory engineering, humanities, and social sciences. In the last two years, most courses are in engineering, usually with a concentration in one branch. Some engineering schools and two-year colleges have agreements that the two-year colleges provide the initial engineering education, and the engineering schools automatically admit students for their last two years. In addition, a few engineering schools have arrangements that students spend three years in a liberal arts college, studying pre-engineering subjects, and two years in an engineering school studying core subjects; students would then receive a bachelor's degree from each school.

Research colleges and universities determine if they offer additional educational incentives. For example, some schools offer cooperative plans that combine classroom study and practical work, permitting students to gain valuable experience and finance part of their education.

LICENSURE

All fifty states and the District of Columbia require licensure for engineers whose work may affect life, health, or property or for engineers who offer their services to the public. Engineers who are licensed are called Professional Engineers (PE). This licensure generally requires a degree from an ABET-accredited engineering program, four years of relevant work experience, and completion of a state examination. Recent graduates can start the licensing process by taking the examination in two stages. The initial examination can be taken upon graduation. Engineers who pass this examination are commonly called Engineers in Training (EIT). The EIT certification is usually valid for ten years. After acquiring suitable work experience, EITs can take the second examination, the Principles and Practice of Engineering Exam. Though PEs must be licensed in each state in which they practice, most states recognize licensure from other states. Many civil, electrical, mechanical, and chemical engineers are certified as PEs.

GETTING STARTED AND ADVANCING

Engineers should be creative, inquisitive, analytical, and detail oriented. They should be able to work as part of a team and be able to communicate well, both orally and in writing. If you possess most or all of these skills, you may excel in this diverse field.

Beginning engineering graduates usually work under the supervision of experienced engineers and, in large companies, may receive formal classroom or seminar-type training. As new engineers gain knowledge and experience, they are assigned more difficult projects with greater independence to develop designs, solve problems, and make decisions. With increasing experience and responsibility, engineers advance to become technical specialists or to supervise a staff or team of engineers and technicians. Some become engineering managers or enter other managerial or sales jobs.

SAMPLE PROGRAM

A search on the Internet or contacting the appropriate professional associations listed in Appendix A will lead you to hundreds of engineering programs. Featured below is a composite program, included to give you an idea of what to expect at the college or university of your choice. As mentioned earlier, programs differ in their emphasis, so investigate each school before making a decision.

Department of Architectural and Civil Engineering

The Department of Architectural and Civil Engineering offers two undergraduate degrees accredited by the Engineering Accreditation Commission (EAC) of the ABET:

1. Bachelor of Science in Civil Engineering (B.S.C.E.)
2. Bachelor of Science in Architectural Engineering (B.S.A.E.)

A B.S./M.S. program leads to B.S. and M.S. degrees in civil engineering in five years. This program is open to exceptional students who are admitted to the graduate program in their junior year. The five-year B.S./M.S. program leads to the following two degrees:

1. B.S./M.S. in Architectural Engineering
2. B.S./M.S. in Civil Engineering

The department offers graduate programs leading to the following degrees:

1. Master of Science in Architectural Engineering (M.S.A.E)
2. Master of Science in Civil Engineering (M.S.C.E.)
3. Doctor of Philosophy (Ph.D.) in Civil Engineering
4. Doctor of Arts (D.A.) in Civil Engineering.

Architectural and Civil Engineering. The goal of the architectural engineering program at the university is to prepare graduates for traditional entry-level positions in the building industry, as well as for graduate programs leading to further specialization in any of the major discipline areas of architectural engineering. The educational objectives of the architectural and civil engineering programs are to produce graduates who (a) have a sound background in the fundamentals of engineering and are prepared to practice architectural engineering in the areas of structures, environmental systems, and construction management, (b) have the abilities and education expected by industry, and (c) are prepared to enter graduate or professional degree programs, as well as other careers.

The architectural engineering curriculum provides an integrated educational experience in mathematics, basic sciences, humanities, social sciences, engineering sciences, and architectural engineering design. The architectural engineering program integrates design applications across the curriculum, beginning with materials and methods of construction, and architectural design in the sophomore year and continuing with structural and building services design in the junior and senior years.

The civil engineering curriculum provides an integrated educational experience in mathematics, basic sciences, humanities, social sciences, engineering sciences, and civil engineering design. The first two years of the civil engineering curriculum are intended to provide a strong foundation in mathematics and basic sciences. During the next two years of the four-year program, the civil engineering curriculum integrates engineering sciences with design applications in the areas of structural, environment, geotechnical, and transportation engineering. The curriculum culminates with a major senior-level design project that includes design applications from the major disciplines of civil engineering.

SALARIES FOR ENGINEERS

Civil/Structural/Architectural Engineers

Median annual earnings were $68,600 in 2006. The middle 50 percent's earnings were between $54,520 and $86,260. The lowest 10 percent earned less than $44,810, and the highest 10 percent earned more than $104,420 annually.

Mean annual earnings in the industries employing the largest numbers of civil, structural, or architectural engineers were as follows:

Industry	Mean annual earnings
Federal government, executive branch	$77,970
Engineering and architectural services	$73,990
Nonresidential building construction	$71,790
Local government	$70,870
State government	$63,000

According to a 2007 salary survey by the National Association of Colleges and Employers (NACE), bachelor's degree candidates in civil engineering received starting offers averaging about $48,509 a year; $48,280 for master's degree candidates in civil engineering; and $62,275 for Ph.D. candidates in civil engineering.

Mechanical Engineers

Median annual earnings of mechanical engineers were $69,850 in 2006. The middle 50 percent earned between $55,420 and $87,550. The lowest 10 percent earned less than $45,170, and the highest 10 percent earned more than $104,900.

Mean annual earnings in the industries employing the largest numbers of mechanical engineers were as follows:

Scientific research and development	$83,240
Federal government, executive branch	$82,310
Navigation, control, and measuring instruments	$78,250
Aerospace and parts manufacturing	$77,210
Engineering and architectural services	$76,630

According to a 2007 NACE salary survey, bachelor's degree candidates in mechanical engineering received starting offers averaging about $54,128 a year; $62,798 for master's degree candidates; and $72,763 for Ph.D. candidates.

Electrical and Electronics Engineers

Median annual earnings of electrical and electronics engineers were $81,050 in 2006. The middle 50 percent earned between $64,440 and $99,630. The lowest 10 percent earned less than $52,050, and the highest 10 percent earned more than $119,900.

Mean annual earnings in the industries employing the largest numbers of electrical and electronics engineers were as follows:

Scientific research and development services	$91,830
Federal government, executive branch	$87,210
Semiconductor and other electronic components	$84,710
Navigation, control, and measuring instruments	$81,800
Engineering and architectural services	$81,630

According to a 2007 NACE salary survey, bachelor's degree candidates in electrical and electronics engineering received starting offers averaging about $55,292 a year; $66,309 for master's degree candidates; and $75,982 for Ph.D. candidates.

JOB OUTLOOK

According to the U.S. Bureau of Labor Statistics (BLS), employment opportunities in engineering are expected to be good through the year 2016. Overall engineering employment is expected to increase about as fast as the average for all occupations, and the number of engineering degrees granted has remained fairly constant over the past several years.

Projected growth varies by specialty, ranging from slower-than-average-growth (4 percent) among electronics, materials, and mechanical engineers to much-faster-than-average growth among biomedical engineers. Competitive pressures and advancing technology will force companies to improve and update product designs more frequently and to optimize their manufacturing processes.

Employers will rely on engineers to increase productivity, as investment in plant and equipment increases to expand output of goods and services. New computer systems have improved the design process, enabling engineers to produce and analyze various product designs more rapidly. Despite these widespread applications, computer technology is not expected to limit employment opportunities.

Finally, additional engineers will be needed to improve or build new roads, bridges, water and pollution control systems, and other public facilities.

Many engineering jobs are related to developing technologies used in national defense. Because defense expenditures—particularly expenditures for aircraft, missiles, and other weapons systems—are not expected to return to previously high levels, the job outlook may be less favorable for engineers working in defense-related fields.

The number of bachelor's degrees awarded in engineering began declining in 1987 and continued to decline through 2005 in the United States. Internationally the number of engineering degrees has increased. Though projecting engineering enrollments is difficult, the total number of graduates from engineering programs is not expected to increase significantly over the projection period. Some engineering schools have restricted enrollments, especially in defense-related fields, such as aerospace engineering, to accommodate the reduced job opportunities.

Though a small proportion of engineers leave the profession each year, many job openings will arise from replacement needs. A greater proportion of replacement openings is created by engineers who transfer to management, sales, or other professional specialty occupations than by those who leave the labor force.

Most industries are less likely to lay off engineers than other workers. Many engineers work on long-term research and development (R&D) projects or in other activities that continue even during economic slowdowns. In industries such as electronics and aerospace, however, large cutbacks in defense expenditures and government R&D funds, as well as the trend toward contracting out engineering work to engineering services firms, have resulted in significant layoffs for engineers.

CONTINUING EDUCATION FOR ENGINEERS

Engineers, like those working in other technical occupations, must continue their education throughout their careers because much of their value to their employer depends on their knowledge of the latest technology. Though the pace of technological change varies by engineering specialty and industry, advances in technology have affected every engineering discipline. Engineers in high-technology areas, such as advanced electronics, may find that technical knowledge can become obsolete rapidly. Even those who continue their education are vulnerable if the technology or product in which they have specialized becomes obsolete. By keeping current in their field, engineers are able to deliver the best solutions and greatest value to their employers. Engineers who have not kept current in their field may find themselves passed over for promotions or vulnerable to layoffs, should they occur. On the other hand, it is often these high-technology areas that offer the greatest challenges, the most interesting work, and the highest salaries. Therefore, the choice of engineering specialty and employer involves an assessment of the potential rewards and of the risk of technological obsolescence.

SAMPLE JOB LISTINGS

These listings are provided as a sample, and as such, the hiring firms are not mentioned. You may find similar listings by doing an Internet search using keywords such as jobs and engineering.

Architectural Engineer, Arizona
A firm active in national and international markets for over fifty-four years has a position for a Registered Architect/Project Manager. Candidate must be a team player with design talent, leadership skills, and approximately ten years of experience in the health-care or educational field. Registration and AutoCAD experience required.

Structural Manager, Colorado
Opportunity for skilled and ambitious engineer. We need motivated, creative self-starters for the structural manager position. Management of staff and ownership opportunity. PE or the ability to become licensed within one year desirable. Experienced wood frame designer, some steel and concrete, for residential and small commercial projects. Experience with design in snow country helpful. This is a challenging position to work with architectural masterpieces. Seven to ten years' experience. Flexible hours, excellent benefits, and top salary. We are a small ten-person office.

Civil/Site Design Engineer, Iowa
One of the top engineering and architectural firms in the country is looking for energetic and creative engineers. As a project engineer,

you will be responsible for site design, planning, and development, as well as roadway, drainage, utilities, and grading. A B.S.C.E. and three to five-plus years' experience required. EIT/PE preferred, as is InRoads and Microstation experience.

Electrical Engineer/PE, Vermont
Must have PE license. Experience in design of LV, MV, and HV power systems. Work includes relaying theory and application, short circuit analysis, load flow analysis. B.S.M.E.-EIT/PE preferred, with five-plus years' experience in design of HVAC, plumbing, and fire protection systems. Commercial and institutional buildings with emphasis on hospital and critical facilities.

FIRSTHAND ACCOUNT

Maggie Shannon Wagenaar, Civil Engineer

Maggie Shannon Wagenaar is the president of her South Florida company, Sunbelt Environmental, which she formed in 1986. She is a registered professional engineer with a bachelor's degree in civil engineering from Virginia Polytechnic Institute and State University.

Getting Started

"I attended Virginia Polytechnic Institute and State University and earned my B.S. in civil engineering technology in 1976. Not surprisingly, I was the only woman in my program, and because of that, I felt isolated at times. The men would get together and study in their dorms or fraternity houses, but I lived at home and had to work alone. And since I was the only woman, I stuck out like a sore thumb. I could never skip a class or slack off because everyone would notice. As a result, I was forced to learn more on my own and become more independent. But I had the support of my professors, and that helped a lot.

"I worked in one department where I was the only registered PE. I put in longer hours than anyone else, I always took work home with me, and yet my salary was the lowest. I could have gone to court dozens of times.

"Discrimination is a way of life for women in this field, especially younger women, but I've seen some women commit professional suicide by pursuing it. If you dwell on it, make a huge issue of it, you can end up being blackballed. Yes, it hurts sometimes, but I think the best course is to ignore it and work as hard as you can to prove them wrong.

"After I graduated, I continued with my plan of hard work. Putting in sixty-hour to eighty-hour weeks for the next ten years, I moved up from junior engineer and project engineer to project manager. And in 1986, I opened my own firm."

What the Work Is Like

"When you're the boss, you call the shots and you do not have to worry about other distracting issues. I can devote my energy to my number one interest, preserving the environment. My main goal is to help keep this world livable, and water purity is one cause with which I'm particularly concerned. It's a precious commodity, and though there are many good laws and regulations to force us to pay attention, many still do not see how precious water really is.

"Sunbelt Environmental is a small firm with anywhere from six to ten employees, depending on current workload. I want to keep it small because I feel that if a company gets too large, then the president ends up spending more time on employee matters than on the outside world. With computer technology—and we utilize all the latest—a small firm can accomplish a lot.

"Running a business is far more demanding than I had realized when I first started out. It has its ups and downs, but it's always challenging and I love it."

Advice from Maggie Shannon Wagenaar

"If you're just starting out and you're a woman, it might help to know that it does get easier as you get older. If you work hard over the years to build a proven track record, one that no one can dispute, meet your deadlines, and show that you have a firm commitment, it really does help to change attitudes. Clients and colleagues will, more often than not, notice your capabilities and not your gender."

URBAN AND REGIONAL PLANNING

Historically, urban planning has been closely associated with architecture. Increasingly, however, planning is concerned with economics, demographics, and public policy as well as land use and community development. Planners perform various tasks, from transportation studies and environmental impact assessments to zoning code analyses.

A few independent planning firms exist, but most planners are employed by larger architecture and engineering firms or at various state and local governmental levels. Many architecture schools offer degree programs in planning, usually at the master's and doctoral levels.

DUTIES

Planners develop long-term and short-term land-use plans to provide for growth and revitalization of urban, suburban, and rural communities, while helping local officials make decisions concerning social, economic, and environmental problems. Because local governments employ the majority of urban and regional planners, they are often referred to as community, regional, or city planners. Planners promote the best use of a community's land and resources for residential, commercial, institutional, and recreational purposes. Planners may be involved in other activities, including decisions on alternative public transportation system plans, resource development, and protection of ecologically sensitive regions. They address issues such as traffic congestion, air pollution, and the effect of growth and change on a community. They may formulate plans relating to the construction of school buildings, public housing, or other infrastructures. Some planners are involved in environmental issues ranging from pollution control to wetland preservation, forest conservation, or the location of new landfills. Planners may be involved with drafting legislation on environmental, social, and economic issues, such as sheltering the homeless, planning a new park, or meeting the demand for new correctional facilities.

Planners examine proposed community facilities such as schools to ensure these facilities will meet the changing demands placed upon them over time. They keep abreast of economic and legal issues involved in zoning codes, building codes, and environmental regulations. They ensure that builders and developers follow these codes and regulations. Planners deal with land-use issues created by population movements. For example, as suburban growth and economic development create more new jobs outside cities, the need for public transportation that enables workers to get to these jobs increases. In response, planners develop transportation models for possible implementation and explain their details to planning boards and the general public.

Before preparing plans for community development, planners report on the current use of land for residential, business, and community purposes. These reports include information on the location and capacity of streets, highways, water and sewer lines, schools, libraries, and cultural and recreational sites. They provide data on the industry types in the community, population characteristics, and employment and economic trends. With this information, along with input from citizens' advisory committees, planners design the layout of land uses for buildings and other facilities, such as subway lines and stations, and prepare reports showing how their programs can be carried out and their cost.

Planners use computers to record and analyze information and to prepare reports and recommendations for government executives and others. Computer databases, spreadsheets, and analytical techniques are used to project program costs and forecast future trends in employment, housing, transportation, or population. Computerized geographic information systems (GIS) enable planners to map land areas and overlay maps with geographic variables, such as population density, and allow them to combine and manipulate geographic information to produce alternative plans for land use or development.

Urban and regional planners often confer with land developers, civic leaders, and public officials. They may function as mediators in community disputes and present alternatives acceptable to opposing parties. Planners may prepare material for community relations programs, speak at civic meetings, and appear before legislative committees and elected officials to explain and defend their proposals.

In large organizations, planners usually specialize in a single area such as transportation, demography, housing, historic preservation, urban design, environmental and regulatory issues, or economic development. In small organizations, planners must be able to do various kinds of planning.

WORKING CONDITIONS FOR PLANNERS

Urban and regional planners are often required to travel to inspect the land features under consideration for development or regulation, including current use and the structures on it. Some local government planners involved in site development inspections spend most of their time in the field. Though most planners have a scheduled forty-hour workweek, they frequently attend evening or weekend meetings or public hearings with citizens' groups. Planners may experience the pressure of deadlines and tight work schedules, as well as political pressure generated by interest groups affected by land-use proposals.

EMPLOYMENT FIGURES

Urban and regional planners held about 34,000 jobs nationwide in 2006, and about seven out of ten are employed by local governments. An increasing proportion of planners work in the private sector for companies involved with architectural, engineering, and related services or with management, scientific, and technical consulting services. Others are employed in state agencies dealing with housing, transportation, or environmental protection and the federal government executive branch.

JOB OUTLOOK

According to the U.S. Bureau of Labor Statistics (BLS), employment of urban and regional planners is expected to grow faster than the average for all occupations through 2016. This growth is a result of the need for state and local governments to provide public services such as regulation of commercial development, the environment, transportation, housing, and land use and development. Nongovernmental initiatives dealing with historic preservation and redevelopment will provide additional openings. Some job openings will arise from the need to replace experienced planners who transfer to other occupations, retire, or leave the labor force for other reasons.

Most planners work for local governments with limited resources and many demands for services. When communities need to cut expenditures, planning services may be cut before more basic services such as police or education. As a result, the number of openings in private industry for consulting positions is expected to grow more rapidly than the number of openings in government.

Most new jobs for urban and regional planners will arise in more affluent, rapidly expanding communities. Local governments need planners to address an array of problems associated with population growth. For example, new housing developments require roads, sewer systems, fire stations, schools, libraries, and recreation facilities that must be planned while considering budgetary constraints. Small town chambers of commerce, economic development authorities, and tourism bureaus may hire planners, preferring candidates with some background in marketing and public relations.

TRAINING FOR PLANNERS

Employers prefer workers who have advanced training. Most entry-level jobs in federal, state, and local government agencies require a master's degree in urban or regional planning, urban design, geography, or a similar course of study. For some positions, a bachelor's degree and related work experience is sufficient. A bachelor's degree from an accredited planning program, coupled with a master's degree in architecture, landscape architecture, or civil engineering, is good preparation for entry-level planning jobs in areas such as urban design, transportation, or the environment.

A master's degree from an accredited planning program provides the best training for a number of planning fields. Though graduates from one of the limited number of accredited bachelor's degree programs qualify for many entry-level positions, their advancement opportunities are often limited unless they acquire an advanced degree.

Courses in related disciplines such as architecture, law, earth sciences, demography, economics, finance, health administration, geographic information systems, and management are highly recommended. In addition, familiarity with computer models and statistical techniques is necessary.

In 2007, about sixty-six colleges and universities offered an accredited master's degree program, and about fifteen offered an accredited bachelor's degree program in urban or regional planning. These programs are accredited by the Planning Accreditation Board, which consists of representatives of the American Institute of Certified Planners (AICP), the American Planning Association (APA), and the Association of Collegiate Schools of Planning. Most graduate programs in planning require a minimum of two years. Specialized courses most commonly offered by planning schools are environmental planning, land use and comprehensive planning, economic development, housing, historic preservation, and social planning. Other popular offerings include community development, transportation, and urban design.

Graduate students spend considerable time in studios, workshops, and laboratory courses learning to analyze and solve planning problems. They often must work in a planning office part-time or during the summer. Local government planning offices frequently offer students internships, providing invaluable experience in obtaining a full-time planning position after graduation.

The AICP, a professional institute within the APA, grants certification to individuals who have the appropriate combination of education and professional experience and pass an examination. Certification may be helpful for promotion.

New Jersey is the only state that requires planners to be licensed, though Michigan requires registration to use the title "community planner."

Planners must be able to think in terms of spatial relationships and visualize the effects of their plans and designs. Planners should be flexible and be able to reconcile different viewpoints and make constructive policy recommendations. The ability to communicate, orally and in writing, is necessary for anyone in this field.

After a few years of experience, planners may advance to assignments requiring a high degree of independent judgment, such as designing the physical layout of a large development or recommending policy and budget options. Some public sector planners are promoted to community planning director and spend much time meeting with officials, speaking to civic groups, and supervising a staff. Further advancement occurs through a transfer to a larger jurisdiction with more complex problems and greater responsibilities or into related occupations, such as director of community or economic development.

SALARIES

Median annual earnings of urban and regional planners were about $56,630 in 2006. The middle 50 percent earned between $44,480 and $71,390 a year. The lowest 10 percent earned less than $35,610, and the highest 10 percent earned more than $86,880 a year. Average (mean) annual earnings for urban and regional planners last year were $56,290 in local government, $57,490 in state government, and $81,820 in federal government.

SAMPLE JOB LISTINGS

These listings are provided as a sample, and as such, the hiring firms are not mentioned. You may find similar listings by visiting the American Society of Landscape Architects (ASLA) website (asla.org).

Urban Designer/Illustrator, Nevada
A major city is seeking an experienced professional to serve in the capacity of Urban Designer/Illustrator with a city growth program. This position will work closely with the Design Officer in visually communicating the application of our growth initiative through three-dimensional, computer-simulated illustrations in the following arenas of urban design:

- Infill and redevelopment ordinance
- New urbanist subdivision principles
- Transit corridor planning and enhancements
- Downtown design guidelines
- Neighborhood design guidelines
- Redevelopment master plan areas

In addition, this position will assist the Growth Officer in creating outreach materials and implementing tools that increase the awareness of the role of urban design and result in creating a more livable city. Qualified candidates will have a bachelor's degree in urban/environmental design, architecture, landscape architecture, or a related field, plus five years of related work experience, two of which were in a lead or supervisory capacity. Proficiency with CAD drawing systems, 3-D projection and rendering software, geographic information systems (GIS), Photoshop, PageMaker, Freehand/Illustrator strongly preferred.
Experience required: five years of relevant experience, two in lead or supervisory role.
Education requirements: bachelor's degree in urban/environmental design, architecture, landscape architecture, or a related field.

Site Planner, New Jersey
Leading architectural and engineering firm has immediate openings for site planners. Individuals need to perform various tasks including zoning research, site analysis and design, base map preparations, and presentation drawings for retail/commercial sites. Position requires a good knowledge of AutoCAD 14, color rendering abilities, good graphic skills, organizational and communication skills. Candidates should be self-starting team players with multitasking abilities to work in a fast-paced environment. We offer a competitive salary, benefits, and bonus package with an opportunity for career growth in a stable environment.
Experience required: one to four years.
Education requirements: a degree from an accredited college or university in planning, landscape architecture, architecture, or civil engineering.

FIRSTHAND ACCOUNT

Matthew I. Zehnder, Landscape Architect/Regional Planner

Matthew I. Zehnder works for META Associates, Inc., a health-care strategic planning and program management firm, in Louisville, Kentucky. He is senior vice president of landscape architecture and community planning. The firm deals primarily with all developmental aspects of health-care projects, from the master planning of health-care assisted-living communities to forty-bed private care facilities.

He earned his Bachelor of Science in Landscape Architecture (B.S.L.A.) from the University of Kentucky in Lexington, Kentucky, in 1988. In 1993, he earned a master's degree in landscape architecture and regional planning from the University of Pennsylvania in Philadelphia.

Getting Started

"I was first attracted to the profession with the thought that I would have opportunities to work outdoors on occasion. I enjoyed working with plants and was interested in learning how to implement a design using plants as a palette.

"I researched several firms in the community where I wanted to live. I learned as much about each firm as possible, including the firms' partners, so when I went on my interviews I could speak intelligently about each firm's accomplishments.

"Eventually, I was approached by a midlevel executive from META Associates, the firm that currently employs me. The person who approached me asked me if I would be interested in leading their planning department. I was interested and began what was to be a six-month interview process.

"I was interviewed by all three partners separately for approximately two hours per interview. I was essentially allowed to espouse my views and ideas concerning design and how I market myself and the firms I had represented.

"After my last individual interview, I was asked to attend a luncheon with all the partners in attendance. They asked me about my specific goals for my career and what I would like to accomplish in my design life.

"After that I was asked to draft a business plan and forecast a figure of billable hours for myself. Following my producing this document was a final interview during which I presented my requirements for employment. Our negotiations following this meeting culminated in a written offer that I accepted."

What the Work Is Like

"My job is the most wonderful job I could have imagined. I set my own hours, within reason. I answer to one partner and am responsible for myself. My job is a little unusual in that I have pursued the marketing and contractual administration path that it seems few landscape architects (LAs) pursue.

"My typical day begins at 9:00 a.m. I listen to my voice mail and promptly answer them all. I write around ten notes to different business associates and friends so that my network line remains open and current. The three most important words here are network, network, network.

"If I am not working on a proposal, then I am completing a schematic design or I am making appointments to visit with people to whom my firm could provide a service.

"I do not spend a lot of time drawing. When I began my LA career, I ran blueprints and mostly did the grunt work, but with hard work and experience, I progressed to executive management.

"My job keeps me moving, locally and nationally, and my workweek averages about sixty-five hours a week. I do not bring work home. My position is corporate, yet I depend on many individuals to assist me in completing my job. That is, I am willing to believe others can do as good a job or better than I can. I travel to the job sites frequently. My firm competes nationally, so I log approximately 120,000 miles a year in the sky. The work atmosphere is user-friendly and open. Everyone freely comments about my design ideas and makes suggestions, when warranted, on ways to improve a design.

"I enjoy the freedom my employer permits me. I enjoy the trust my employer puts in me, and I enjoy the varied design professionals with whom I interact. The least enjoyable part of my job is the paperwork and the complicated time-sheet processes."

Advice from Matthew I. Zehnder

"Know what you want to do and where you want to be throughout the course of your life. It is essential to write down a set of goals to reach in five years and continue to review your goals and adjust them as necessary. In this field, you must decide between the academic world and the professional world of this profession. They are two different worlds, so you should thoroughly research each area. Pick the firm you want to work for and pursue it as if it's the last place in the world to work. And the most important item is to believe in what you want to do and then do it."

CONSTRUCTION AND COST ESTIMATION

Some architects move into careers in construction, working as contractors, construction managers, cost estimators, or providers of design/build services. These careers require experience in materials and products and their costs; labor and labor relations; construction planning and logistics; and construction equipment, scheduling, and operations.

DUTIES OF CONSTRUCTION MANAGERS

Construction managers assume many responsibilities and positions within construction firms and are known by a range of job titles, often used interchangeably. For example, a construction manager may be known as a construction superintendent, general superintendent, project manager, general construction manager, or executive construction manager.

Construction managers may be owners or salaried employees of a construction management or contracting firm, or they may be individuals working under contract or as salaried employees for the owner, developer, contractor, or management firm overseeing the construction project. We'll use the term construction manager to encompass all supervisory-level salaried and self-employed construction managers who oversee construction supervisors and workers.

In the construction industry, managers and other professionals active in the industry—general managers, project engineers, cost estimators, and others—are increasingly referred to as constructors. The term constructor refers to a broad group of professionals in construction who, through education and experience, are capable of managing, coordinating, and supervising the construction process from conceptual development through final construction on a timely and economical basis. With designs for buildings, roads, bridges, or other projects, constructors oversee the organization, scheduling, and implementation of the projects to execute those designs. They are responsible for coordinating and managing people, materials, and equipment; budgets, schedules, and contracts; and the safety of employees and the general public.

The term construction manager is used more narrowly within the construction industry to denote a firm, or an individual employed by the firm, involved in management oversight of a construction project. Under this narrower definition, construction managers generally act as agents or representatives of the owner or developer throughout the life of the project. Though they generally play no direct role in the actual construction of the building or other facility, they typically schedule and coordinate all design and construction processes. They develop and implement a management plan to complete the project according to the owner's goals that allows the design and construction processes to be carried out efficiently and effectively within budgetary and schedule constraints.

Generally, a contractor is the firm under contract to provide specialized construction services. On small projects such as remodeling a home, the construction contractor is usually a self-employed construction manager or skilled trade worker who directs and oversees employees. On larger projects, construction managers working for a general contractor have overall responsibility for completing the construction in accordance with the engineer's or architect's drawings and specifications and prevailing building codes. They arrange for subcontractors to perform specialized craft work or other specified construction work.

Large construction projects, such as an office building or industrial complex, for example, are too complicated for one person to supervise. These projects are divided into many segments:

- Site preparation, including land clearing and earthmoving
- Sewage systems
- Landscaping and road construction

- Building construction, including excavation and laying foundations, erection of structural framework, floors, walls, and roofs
- Building systems, including fire protection, electrical, plumbing, air-conditioning, and heating

Construction managers may work as part of a team or may be in charge of one or more of these activities. They may have several subordinates, such as assistant project managers, superintendents, field engineers, or crew supervisors, reporting to them.

Construction managers plan, budget, and direct the construction project. They evaluate various construction methods and determine the most cost-effective plan and schedule. They determine the appropriate construction methods and schedule all required construction site activities into logical, specific steps, budgeting the time required to meet established deadlines. This may require sophisticated estimating and scheduling techniques, using computers with specialized software. Construction managers determine the labor requirements and, in some cases, supervise or monitor the hiring and dismissal of workers.

Managers direct and monitor the progress of field or site construction activities, at times through other construction supervisors. This includes the delivery and use of materials, tools, and equipment and includes the quality of construction, worker productivity, and safety. They are responsible for obtaining all necessary permits and licenses and, depending upon the contractual arrangements, direct or monitor compliance with building and safety codes and other regulations.

They regularly review engineering and architectural drawings and specifications to monitor progress and ensure compliance with plans and specifications. They track and control construction costs to avoid cost overruns. Based on direct observation and reports by subordinate supervisors, managers may prepare daily reports of progress and requirements for labor, material, and machinery and equipment at the construction site.

Construction managers work out of a main office from which the overall construction project is monitored or out of a field office at the construction site. Though construction managers meet regularly with owners, subcontractors, architects, and other design professionals to monitor and coordinate all construction project phases, management decisions regarding daily construction activities are usually made at the job site. Managers usually travel when the construction site is in another state or when they are responsible for activities at two or more sites. Management of construction projects overseas usually entails temporary residence in another country.

Construction managers must be on call to address issues arising from bad weather, site delays, and emergencies. Most work more than a forty-hour week since construction may proceed around-the-clock. This type of work schedule can go on for days, even weeks, to meet special project deadlines, especially if unforeseen delays have occurred.

Though the work generally is not considered dangerous, construction managers must be careful while touring construction sites, especially when large machinery, heavy equipment, and vehicles are being operated. Managers must be able to establish priorities and assign duties. They need to observe job conditions and to be alert to changes and potential problems, particularly involving safety on the job site and adherence to regulations.

TRAINING FOR CONSTRUCTION MANAGERS

Students may pursue baccalaureate or advanced degrees in building sciences, construction science, construction management, or civil engineering. Some of these programs are offered in architecture schools, others in engineering or separate construction schools. The American Council for Construction Education (ACCE) accredits academic programs in construction.

People interested in becoming construction managers need a solid background in building science, business, and management, as well as related work experience within the construction industry. They need to understand contracts, plans, and specifications, and they need to be knowledgeable about construction methods, materials, and regulations. Familiarity with computers and software programs for job costing, scheduling, and estimating has become increasingly important.

Traditionally, people advance to construction management positions after having substantial experience as construction craft workers (for example, carpenters, masons, plumbers, or electricians) or after having worked as construction supervisors or as owners of independent specialty contracting firms overseeing workers in one or more construction trades.

However, more employers, particularly large construction firms, hire individuals who combine industry work experience with a bachelor's degree in construction, building science, or construction management. Practical industry experience is important, whether through internships, cooperative education programs, or industry tenure.

In 2006, 105 colleges and universities offered four-year degree programs in construction management or construction science. These programs include courses in project control and development, site planning, design, construction methods, construction materials, value analysis, cost estimating, scheduling, contract administration, accounting, business and financial management, safety, building codes and standards, inspection procedures, engineering and architectural sciences, mathematics, statistics, and information technology.

Graduates from four-year degree programs are usually hired as assistants to project managers, field engineers, schedulers, or cost estimators. An increasing number of graduates in related fields, for example engineering or architecture, enter construction management, often after having had substantial experience on construction projects or having completed graduate studies in construction management or building science.

Around sixty colleges and universities offer a master's degree program in construction management or construction science, and at least two offer a Ph.D. in the field. Master's degree recipients, especially those with work experience in construction, typically become construction managers in large construction or construction management companies. Often, individuals who hold a bachelor's degree in an unrelated field seek a master's degree to work in the construction industry. Doctoral degree recipients usually become college professors or conduct research.

CERTIFICATION FOR CONSTRUCTION MANAGERS

The American Institute of Constructors (AIC) and the Construction Management Association of America (CMAA) have established voluntary certification programs for construction professionals. Requirements combine written examinations with verification of professional experience. AIC awards the designations Associate Constructor (AC) and Certified Professional Constructor (CPC) to candidates who meet set requirements and pass appropriate construction examinations. CMAA awards the designation Certified Construction Manager (CCM) to practitioners who meet the requirements in a construction management firm, complete a professional construction management capstone course, and pass a technical examination. Though certification is not required to work in the construction industry, voluntary certification can be valuable because it provides evidence of competence and experience. There is a growing movement toward certification in this industry to serve as evidence of competence and experience.

SALARIES FOR CONSTRUCTION MANAGERS AND CONTRACTORS

Earnings of salaried construction managers and self-employed independent construction contractors vary depending upon the size and nature of the construction project, its geographic location, and economic conditions. In addition to typical benefits, many salaried construction managers receive bonuses and the use of company motor vehicles.

Median annual earnings of construction managers (except those who were self-employed) in 2006 were $73,700. The middle 50 percent earned between $56,090 and $98,350. The lowest 10 percent earned less than $43,210, and the highest 10 percent earned more than $135,780 annually. Median annual earnings in the industries employing the largest numbers of managers were as follows:

Building equipment contractors	$75,200
Electrical contractors	$74,380
Nonresidential building construction	$74,080
Foundation, structure, and exterior building	$71,640
Residential building construction	$69,400

According to a 2007 National Association of Colleges and Employers (NACE) salary survey, candidates with a bachelor's degree in construction management or construction science received offers averaging $46,930 a year.

JOB OUTLOOK FOR CONSTRUCTION MANAGERS

Construction managers held about 487,000 jobs nationwide in 2006. Around 277,590 of them were self-employed. About 83 percent of salaried construction managers are employed in the construction industry. Within the construction industry, about 36 percent are employed by specialty trade contractors (for example, plumbing, heating and air-conditioning, and electrical contractors), about 50 percent by building construction contractors, and about 14 percent by heavy and civic engineering construction contractors. Engineering, architectural, and construction management services firms, as well as local governments, educational institutions, and real estate developers, employed the other 17 percent of construction managers.

According to the U.S. Bureau of Labor Statistics (BLS), employment of construction managers is expected to increase faster than the average for all occupations through 2016, as the level and complexity of construction activity continues to grow. Employment opportunities are considered excellent because job growth is expected to exceed the number of qualified graduates through 2016. Prospects in construction management, engineering and architectural services, and construction contracting firms should be best for people who have a bachelor's or higher degree in construction science, construction management, or construction engineering as well as practical experience working in construction.

Employers prefer applicants with previous construction work experience who can combine a strong background in building technology with proven supervisory or managerial skills. In addition to job growth, many openings should result annually from the need to replace workers who transfer to other occupations or leave the labor force.

The increasing complexity of construction projects should raise demand for management-level personnel within the construction industry, as sophisticated technology and the proliferation of laws setting standards for buildings and construction materials, worker safety, energy efficiency, and environmental protection have complicated the construction process. Advances in building materials and construction methods and the growing number of multipurpose buildings, electronically operated "smart" buildings, and energy-efficient structures will further add to the demand for more construction managers. However, employment of construction managers can be sensitive to the short-term nature of many construction projects and cyclical fluctuations in construction activity.

DUTIES OF COST ESTIMATORS

Accurately forecasting the cost of future projects is vital to the survival of any business. Cost estimators develop cost information for owners or managers to use in determining resource and material quantities, making bids for contracts, determining if a new product will be profitable, or which products are making a profit for a firm.

Regardless of the industry in which they work, estimators compile and analyze data on all the factors that can influence costs, such as materials, labor, location, and special machinery requirements, including computer hardware and software. Job duties vary depending on the project's type and size. Cost engineers usually have an engineering background and apply scientific principles and methods to undertake feasibility studies, value engineering, and life-cycle costing. Because computers play an integral role in cost estimating, they should possess strong computer skills. Estimating may involve complex mathematical calculations and require advanced mathematical techniques.

Construction cost estimators may be employed by the project's architect or owner to estimate costs or track actual costs relative to bid specifications as the project develops. In large construction companies employing more than one estimator, estimators commonly specialize. For instance, one may estimate only electrical work and another may concentrate on excavation, concrete, and forms.

TRAINING FOR COST ESTIMATORS

Entry requirements for cost estimators vary by industry. In the construction industry, employers increasingly prefer individuals with a degree in building construction, construction management, or construction science. However, most construction estimators have considerable construction experience, gained through industry tenure, internships, or cooperative education programs. Applicants have a competitive edge if they have a thorough knowledge of construction materials, costs, and procedures in areas ranging from heavy construction to electrical work, plumbing systems, or masonry work.

Cost estimators should have an aptitude for mathematics, be able to analyze, compare, and interpret detailed and sometimes poorly defined information, and make sound and accurate judgments based on this knowledge. Assertiveness and self-confidence in presenting and supporting their conclusions are important, as are strong communication and interpersonal skills, because estimators may work as part of a project team alongside managers, owners, engineers, and design professionals. Cost estimators need knowledge of computers, including word processing and spreadsheet packages. In some instances, familiarity with special estimation software or programming skills may be required.

Regardless of their background, estimators receive much training on the job as each company has its own way of handling estimates. Working with an experienced estimator, they become familiar with each step in the process. Those with no experience reading construction specifications or blueprints first learn that work aspect. They may accompany an experienced estimator to the construction site or shop floor where they will observe the work being done, take measurements, or perform other routine tasks. As they become more knowledgeable, estimators learn how to tabulate quantities and dimensions from drawings and how to select the appropriate material prices.

For most estimators, advancement takes the form of higher pay and prestige. Some move into management positions, such as project manager for a construction firm or manager of the industrial engineering department for a manufacturer. Others may go into business for themselves as consultants, providing estimating services for a fee to government or construction and manufacturing firms.

Many colleges and universities include cost estimating as part of bachelor's and associate degree curriculums in civil engineering, industrial engineering, and construction management or construction engineering technology. In addition, cost estimating is a significant part of many master's degree programs in construction science or construction management. Organizations representing cost estimators, such as the American Association of Cost Engineers (AACE) International and the Society of

Cost Estimating and Analysis (SCEA), sponsor educational and professional development programs. These programs help students, estimators-in-training, and experienced estimators stay abreast of changes affecting the profession. Specialized courses and programs in cost estimating techniques and procedures are offered by many technical schools, community colleges, and universities.

CERTIFICATION FOR COST ESTIMATORS

Voluntary certification can be valuable to cost estimators because it provides professional recognition of the estimator's competence and experience. In some instances, individual employers may require professional certification for employment. Both AACE International and the SCEA administer certification programs. To become certified, estimators usually must have between three and seven years of estimating experience and must pass a written and an oral examination. In addition, certification requirements may include publication of at least one article or paper in the field.

SALARIES FOR COST ESTIMATORS

Salaries of cost estimators vary widely by experience, education, size of firm, and industry. Median annual earnings of cost estimators in 2006 were $52,940. The middle 50 percent earned between $40,320 and $69,460. The lowest 10 percent earned less than $31,600, and the highest 10 percent earned more than $88,310 annually. Median annual earnings in the industries employing the largest numbers of managers were as follows:

Nonresidential building construction	$60,870
Building equipment	$56,170
Foundation, structure, and building exterior	$52,520
Residential building construction	$52,460
Building finishing	$51,610

College graduates with degrees in fields such as engineering or construction management that provide a strong background in cost estimating could start at a higher level than those cited above.

According to a 2007 NACE salary survey, bachelor's degree candidates with degrees in construction science or construction management received offers averaging about $46,930 a year.

JOB OUTLOOK FOR COST ESTIMATORS

Cost estimators held about 221,000 jobs nationwide in 2006; about 62 percent of those are in the construction industry. Another 15 percent of salaried cost estimators were employed in manufacturing industries. The remainder work for engineering and architectural services firms, business services firms, and throughout other industries.

Overall employment of cost estimators is expected to grow faster than the average for all occupations through the year 2016. No new projects in construction, manufacturing, or other industries are undertaken without careful analysis and estimation of the costs involved. In addition to openings created by growth, some job openings will arise from the need to replace workers who transfer to other occupations or leave the labor force.

Growth of the construction industry, where more than half of all cost estimators are employed, will be the driving force behind the demand for these workers. The fastest growing sectors of the construction industry are expected to be special trade contractors and those associated with heavy construction and spending on the nation's infrastructure. Construction and repair of highways, streets, and bridges and construction of more subway systems, airports, water and sewage systems, electric power plants, and transmission lines will stimulate demand for many more cost estimators. Job prospects in construction should be best for cost estimators with a degree in construction management or construction science, engineering, or architecture who have practical experience in various phases of construction or in a specialty craft area.

Employment of cost estimators in manufacturing should remain relatively stable as firms continue to use their services to identify and control their operating costs. Experienced estimators with degrees in engineering, science, mathematics, business administration, or economics and who have computer expertise should have the best job prospects in manufacturing.

SAMPLE JOB LISTING

This listing is provided as a sample, and as such, the hiring firm is not mentioned. You may find similar listings by doing an Internet search using keywords such as jobs, construction, or contracting.

> **Estimators and Senior Contracting, California**
> Estimators who are experienced in mid-rise and high-rise buildings are needed to develop conceptual designs, form costs, prepare firm fixed-price bids, and perform material scheduling and planning for precast wall systems. You will meet with architects, owners, and general contractors, so your experience with precast concrete and a civil engineering degree with ten to twenty years' experience is most helpful.

FIRSTHAND ACCOUNTS

Lee Sullivan Hill, Cost Estimator

Lee Sullivan Hill works for Turner Construction Company, an international construction management and general contracting firm headquartered in New York City. Lee worked in the Washington, D.C., office for seven years, in Connecticut for two years, and is now in Chicago, Illinois.

Getting Started

"As a child, I had never met an engineer. I did not even know what one was. I did, however, love architecture. My grandmother's father had been an 'architect,' and time spent on walks with her taught me to look for mansard roofs and Doric columns by age five.

"Fast-forward to my freshman year in college. My roommate was an engineering student, and I became intrigued by her homework assignments since they looked so interesting. I had always been good at math and interested in architecture, so I decided, three weeks into my sophomore year, to switch to an engineering concentration. The AB engineering program at Lafayette allowed me to take civil engineering courses such as Structures and Design of Small Dams as well as art classes, history, English, and French.

"I had planned to go to graduate school for architecture, but my husband-to-be graduated two years before I did and went to work with Turner Construction. I loved hearing about his job, which was building a dormitory at Gallaudet College in D.C. By the time May rolled around, I had found my niche. I received offers from other construction firms but chose Turner.

"I started with Turner right out of college, and my first assignments were on construction job sites where I was assigned to the cost estimating department. I left to become a stay-at-home mom for several years. When I returned to work, I resumed my estimating duties on a part-time, hourly basis. I have done one estimate for Turner since moving to Chicago in April of 1996 because my other career, writing children's books, has accelerated.

"The training at Turner took me through work on job sites, but I naturally gravitated toward estimating. Even on my first job, where I laid out concrete for a water treatment plant, I did take-off and labor studies. My work was neat, organized, and thorough.

"The training within estimating was mostly one-on-one with my boss. The department had four people in it and included the chief, so I had plenty of time for this method. My natural talents for organizing information made the learning simple. In 1982, when I started, computers were not yet a factor. However, it became my job in 1985 and 1986 to computerize the department and provide training to the other estimators. My boss started me out counting doorframes and windows, and pretty soon I was taking on small projects of my own.

"Turner Construction has a formalized training program of seminars that contributed greatly to my knowledge, while reading trade journals and talking with subcontractors about their work added finishing touches."

What the Work Is Like

"All estimators spend time reviewing drawings and specifications for upcoming construction projects. They study the plans, read the specs, take notes on unusual (maybe expensive) details, make lists of questions and qualifications, and envision the finished building. They might ask themselves, What problems will arise during construction? What has the architect left out of the design that will be needed to finish the work? Can we change some details that will save the owner money and still provide a quality building? Do some details exist that we know cause major problems (such as rainwater seeping through bad flashing details) and to which we should pay attention?

"Secondly, all estimators count. They use digitizers that count with computer programs or they count with their fingers, but all estimators must figure out, for each project, how many square feet, cubic yards, or linear feet are required. This computation must be done in an organized fashion, and it must be checked and rechecked.

"Thirdly, all estimators assign prices to the work. For every item they counted, they assign a price. This is more complicated than you may imagine. It's not just running to a fat book and pulling out a price. Every job has specifics that may make prices higher or lower. For example, one must consider if the work will take place during the winter and require extra money for heat, if new labor contracts coming up might change the costs of the whole project, or consider insurance requirements. They must compare all the details. Subcontractors can offer advice over the phone, and discussions with the owner and architect may clarify unknowns.

"This brings us to the most important task of all: communication. All the organized notes, careful pricing, and checking and rechecking of work are nothing without communication. Final reports, or lump sum bids, or meetings with owners before construction starts, are all critical components of an estimator's job.

"On large projects, the estimate is broken into pieces and assigned to several estimators. The lead estimator must communicate with everyone and pull the information together without dropping a piece that might cost big money later. The ability to communicate is hard to train into people. Companies look for this quality in all of those hired.

"In summary, estimating is a fun, stimulating, exciting process that involves seemingly opposite activities—individual activities such as thinking and counting and group activities that require communication with others, such as contacting subcontractors, owners, architects, and people within your own company. This job is never boring."

The Upsides and Downsides

"I loved seeing plans for new buildings, imagining their beauty, imagining the smell of the concrete foundations freshly poured, the wood floors freshly varnished.

"The only real downside was that sometimes you'd bust your gut for a month on a project and put in a price/bid and find out that another contractor was given the job for a million dollars less than you projected."

Advice from Lee Sullivan Hill

"Study civil engineering, construction management, or architecture in college. Get as much work experience related to the field as you can during the summers. Even being a laborer on a job site counts as construction experience when you look for your job at graduation. And hone your written and verbal communication skills. They will serve you better than anything you could write in your resume."

Steve Lazarian, Licensed General Contractor

Steve Lazarian is owner and president of CityWorks, Inc., located in Pasadena, California. In 1970, he earned his B.A. in economics and business from Westmont College in Montecito, California, and in 1973, he earned his law degree from Cal Western School of Law in San Diego, California. He is a licensed real estate broker and has been in the field since 1972.

Getting Started

"I grew up in a construction atmosphere. My father started an electrical construction business in 1948. As a kid, I swept the warehouse. Later, I worked in purchasing, estimating, and accounting in the office. The business became successful, but I was not interested in the technical aspects, so I went to law school. After graduating, passing the bar, and starting my own practice, I realized that I was most interested in construction law. I developed a clientele with contractors, subcontractors, developers, and real estate brokers.

"After my appointment to the Contractor's State License Board in 1985, I became interested in the business itself. Our family started a general construction business in 1983 that became successful and grew quickly. In 1989, I decided to leave my practice and manage the general construction company, called Crown City Construction, which was liquidated in 1995. That same year I established my own construction company called CityWorks, Inc.

"My training came from my business degree, law degree, the practice of law, serving on the Contractor's Board, and working in my father's business."

What the Work Is Like

"My duties include overseeing the jobs we construct and the management of construction projects, some of which we perform services for before construction commences. I usually start my day by outlining my priorities of what I need to accomplish. This includes confirming meetings and responsibilities of other staff members. I spend much of my time preparing spreadsheets, writing contracts, communicating with subcontractors, authorizing payments to subs and vendors, visiting job sites, and working with owners, architects, engineers, and related parties.

"Construction is a high-risk business. You cannot afford to relax at any time. You have no time to even be busy-relaxed. I need every moment of the day to stay on top of the many pitfalls that can cause one to fail in this business. That is one reason I am extremely organized. That allows me to cover the numerous project-related items that need attention. Each construction job is like operating a separate business because it requires all of the effort and energy of running multiple businesses simultaneously. That keeps the pace fast and exciting and, of course, the personal reward at the job's conclusion is seeing the structure that you have built in its completed form.

"The business of construction is interesting. When we took over the construction of the Los Angeles Mission in downtown Los Angeles from the contractor who had failed on the job, we realized the need for construction management and preconstruction services. We started to render those services in earnest during the past seven years, and it has proven to be the most interesting aspect of the work. We are able to assist the owners during the planning stage, which saves them money and time. That allows us to be professional in an industry that is not professional."

The Upsides and Downsides

"The most rewarding part of the business is helping people meet their needs in planning and building structures for them. In this people-oriented business, you are constantly talking to people all day, every day, so you must be able to work with people. You need to possess team spirit because you perform your work along with many others.

"The ability to communicate is a necessary skill in this field. Since my background and training is in communication and leading effectively by written and spoken word, I enjoy this part of the business.

"The worst part of this business is the dishonesty within the industry. Many companies do not care how they get a job or what it takes to convince an owner of their abilities. They will lie, cheat, and steal to convince an owner to give them the work. Many of these unscrupulous contractors could make as much money by being honest, but dishonesty seems to be endemic in the business."

Advice from Steve Lazarian

"My advice to someone who wants to get into the business is to obtain a degree in construction management, engineering, or a similar field. Even a degree in communications or literature would be helpful because any degree that trains you to be able to write and communicate will give you an advantage.

"You must possess people skills, and you should be able to react to situations quickly. If you are interested in the field, you obviously need physical skills.

"If management is a goal, a graduate degree in law, business management, or finance would be helpful. There has been little consolidation of businesses within the construction industry, mainly because management sophistication is not there. Once that changes, the industry will need more skilled management personnel with graduate degrees. At the entry level, you will need education and experience. The sooner you get that, the easier it will be to get started in the business. So, while going to school, you might consider working part-time for a construction company or taking an internship during the summer vacation periods."

MORE FIRSTHAND ACCOUNTS FROM THE FIELD

To get a good idea of what life is like on a daily basis for those working in the exciting and diverse field of architecture, professionals from a range of backgrounds have been interviewed for this book. You will read about men and women working on large-scale industrial projects and custom homes for individual families. These professionals came to this industry in various unique and interesting ways. They offer words of advice to those considering entering this field that you should consider.

We wish you the best of luck in establishing a successful and satisfying career in the field of architecture.

Jasper (Joe) Hardesty, Architect

Jasper (Joe) Hardesty is the owner of his own firm, Ecotecture, in Albuquerque, New Mexico. He's involved in commercial and institutional architecture, as well as urban planning. He earned his B.S. in architectural studies from the University of Illinois at Urbana-Champaign and has been working in the field since 1981.

Getting Started

"It was always my intention to enter a field involving science. I was strongly encouraged by my instructors in high school to pursue my aptitude in the fine arts. I decided upon architecture as a synthesis of the two: providing opportunity for creativity and expression, while presenting a discipline that solved problems and had practical applications.

"The concept of working with others to generate ideas and environments that people would interact with on a regular basis was particularly stimulating. If we can recognize the social and personal levels in our built environment that influence us, a large number of people over a significant time can derive considerable benefit.

"My first job was not with an architectural firm. At the time I graduated, the fields of architecture and construction in the Midwest and the eastern part of the United States were experiencing a depression. Most firms were laying people off and not hiring or even accepting applications.

"My first related employment was with a consulting engineer who specialized in mechanical/plumbing/electrical engineering. I was offered that position after looking for a job for six months, then responding to an ad from the engineer. My interview involved discussions of my education and expectations of employment, then an exam for production drafting, administered by an associate of the firm.

"My current work is as a self-employed sole proprietor. I chose this path after being approached by several different clients; they had work they wanted me to do, but only if I would do so independently. Because I did not want to be involved with any conflict of interest involving the firm I was working for, I resigned that position and began my own practice. I decided to do this for personal and professional reasons, including a desire to be my own boss, my intent to spend more time with my family, and to pursue planning and architectural interests of my choosing, rather than those of a firm."

What the Work Is Like

"As sole proprietor of a practice, I am the person responsible for decisions regarding all facets of projects, as well as the business. For the business, this means maintaining contacts for possible work, reviewing and administrating contracts, maintaining books for accounting, paying taxes, filing and preparing registration forms, making travel arrangements, billing/collecting from clients, and paying consultants.

"For each project, I am responsible for maintaining budgets and schedules, conceptual development, master planning and land-use, programming of facilities, developing designs, creating graphic material, coordinating with clients and all consultants, verifying compliance with building and zoning codes, administrating the design and document processes, generating and reviewing construction documents, completing specifications, preparing bid documents and conducting the bidding process, administrating construction contracts, site surveys of work under construction, and postoccupancy evaluation of completed work.

"All my projects over the past five years have been focused on sustainable design, which means I work with clients who have an interest in design and construction that has minimal negative impact on the natural and social environment. Most work has involved planning and development of ecotourism facilities, such as small-scale lodges and hotels developed with the intent to preserve natural environments and habitats through tourism revenues. I have been involved in individual homes and subdivision plans for clients who wish to apply environmentally friendly means to residential development.

"All of my work with private firms involves large commercial and institutional projects, including retail stores and malls, factories, housing subdivisions, campus master plans, educational buildings for universities and public schools, medical facilities, museums, offices, and hotels.

"The job is difficult, though the work satisfaction is considerable, even exhilarating. This field requires extensive hours within a discipline that provides little financial reward, so unless you have good business sense and intend to spend much of your time working, you will not make a large amount of money.

"I get up early in the morning (5:00 to 6:00 a.m.) so I can call prospective clients on the East Coast, where it is two hours later than in Albuquerque. I will make as many contact calls to generate new business as possible, then follow up each with a letter and other information that may apply specifically to them. I check messages and e-mail to see what current crisis some client or consultant may be having.

"About every other day, some emergency will occur. If no crisis occurs, I check publications and information resources to maintain my technical library and to look for other potential clients and consultants. There will usually be a meeting or two during the day with clients and/or consultants. I will check on the status of projects under construction, visit a job site, and process a pay request from a contractor. There will often be a need for clarifications and/or changes in documents for work that is out to bid or under construction.

"If I am lucky, I will get to do some work on a newer project in the afternoon or prepare some renderings and information for a presentation. I often must call prospective clients on the West Coast midday to catch them in the morning, then call the East Coast again in the afternoon before they finish for the day, then the West Coast again closer to 5:00 p.m. before they finish.

"The primary use of my time is for communicating and coordinating with others. By evening, I can do some of my own work. I will prepare a list of people to contact and work to be done to prepare for the next day. Depending on project schedules, I will work on project design or construction documents. I will check the work of consultants, review contracts, prepare paperwork, pay bills, and maintain financial records. I will review the unpaid statements sent to clients, then send new statements and note to call them the next day.

"One reason I started in architecture was because of the challenge of making an art form that was functional. In this respect, the work is interesting. I have never been bored by architecture, and I like the aspect of being creative one minute, being an administrator the next, and then a technician after that.

"As a sole proprietor, there is no point in counting hours per week; it would be in the range of eighty to one hundred, with an occasional day off (no weekends). When I worked with other firms, from being an intern to a project manager, the typical workweek was about sixty hours per week, and many were between eighty and one hundred, frequently pulling all-nighters to get work done by deadlines.

"This is a good time to mention that the architectural profession has functioned as an intern-based profession, and it has long maintained the attitude that until interns become professionals, they should pay their dues to earn the status of architect. Once one becomes an architect, then the architect is a professional, working on a salary basis without overtime pay or compensation. This is obviously not true of all firms, but it is prevalent."

Advice from Jasper (Joe) Hardesty

"I would advise anyone considering this career to learn about business. It will help you if you have one, and it will help you to promote yourself within a firm if you choose to do that. Since the profession has become more specialized, you should decide what type of work you want to do, determine if there will be a demand for it, and then pursue that specialty. Start out working with a large firm, which will usually establish a better initial wage for you and will expose you more to the business and practice of architecture. Explore the requirements for registration and licensing as an architect. The requirements have become more demanding. It is more similar to becoming a doctor and less like becoming a lawyer. Get to know some people experienced in architecture. This does not include professors who are paid by having you as a student. Instead, talk to people who are working in architecture, preferably doing what you might like. Recognize that few architects do design work, though I have been fortunate to do a good deal of this in my practice.

"The qualities you should possess include ambition, passion for hard work, excellent communication skills, excellent mediation skills (consultant and contractor administrations are often adversarial), the ability to work and produce under stress, self-confidence (criticism is the norm in the design field), the ability to be creative, and intelligence."

Harvey Schorr, Architect

Harvey Schorr is vice president of Maguire Group Inc., an architectural firm in Foxborough, Massachusetts. He earned his B.Arch. in 1966 and his M.Arch. in advanced studies (urban design) in 1972, both from MIT in Cambridge, Massachusetts. He has been working in the field for thirty five years.

Getting Started

"I used to draw buildings and airplanes as a kid and even remember doing a report on architecture as a career choice in junior high school, so I guess my interest is long-standing. On the other hand, I was intimidated by the prospect of pursuing it, for fear I was not artistic enough. I studied two years of engineering, and that convinced me I wasn't technical enough either. I naively thought airplanes were designed as a sort of visual or aesthetic undertaking. So, since I was at a technical university, I tried architecture somewhat out of desperation. If that hadn't worked out, I would have had to go to law school.

"After spending two years as an undergraduate in aeronautics and astronautics, I decided I needed a change and, by virtue of drafting skills, got a job in an architect's office. That was in the summer of 1962. I was not of much use, but the man who gave me that job, Howard Dutkin, obviously felt some obligation to the next generation. It was a small office with just one other person. As my first assignment, he paid me to sit down and trace drawings for a house that had been completed, and I helped out bordering sheets, running prints, and the like. By the next summer, perhaps as a result of his generosity, he was out of business, but with a year of architectural school to supplement my meager office experience, I was able to get an intern-level job elsewhere.

"To land my current job, I had to be laid off from my previous job. I wasn't a bad employee; the office just ran out of work. This cycle of boom and bust, feast or famine, is little understood or appreciated by many people considering architectural careers.

"It seems like a lifetime that I've been in architecture. Included in the thirty-five years I've been in this field are two years of graduate school, one-and-a-half years in Italy researching small towns as a Fulbright grantee, about eight years of teaching on a part-time basis, two years as a research assistant at the Joint Center for Urban Studies investigating measures of housing quality, and interludes building kilns and helping to start a non-profit center for pottery."

What the Work Is Like

"We are Renaissance people, and we like to think we can do anything. Of course, there are some specialized things we are not well equipped to do—hospitals, clean rooms, high-end retail, for example—and others we don't want to do, such as single-family houses. Everything in between is fair game. Our work is oriented toward commercial, institutional, industrial, and transportation-related projects, with lots of renovation to boot.

"I work on many projects, but as a manager, I am more involved in organizing them than in doing them. That means proposals, contracts, meetings, phone calls, letters, reports, coordination, critiquing, billing, and chasing accounts receivable.

"The work can be interesting and even challenging. It is great when things go smoothly, but that doesn't happen spontaneously. A smooth operation takes hard work and luck, and sometimes even those are not enough.

"People do not realize how much of architecture is not about drawing pretty pictures. It is more like being a banker than being an artist. An artist must answer only to himself in seeking to realize his or her vision.

Architecture, more often than not, is about the bottom line, profit, and return on investment. (Some suggest that bankers do more to shape the built environment than architects.)

"Unfortunately, people, for the most part, are not taught how to do the things that have to be done to run an office or a project. They are ill-equipped in terms of training, and by temperament, to be jacks-of-all-trades, yet that, in a word, is what the job requires. People who cannot write are severely handicapped in carrying out the myriad nontechnical tasks architects must perform.

"That brings me to another issue, namely to the design process, which is, after all, what we are supposed to be doing. Architectural design is typically taught in a way that is comparable to waiting for lightning to strike: you sit around hoping an idea will come, and then you run with it. Only when you've invested a lot of time do you discover that the idea perhaps was the wrong one. I am interested in using rational methods to define problems, generate alternative solutions, evaluate them in objective ways, and make appropriate choices regarding their implementation. Architectural schools have failed, in my opinion, in giving students the basic intellectual tools they need to be productive and successful.

"In general, architects, unlike engineers, do not work by the clock, and may not always be compensated for the work they do. I typically work nine to ten hours per day and all too often six or seven days a week."

Upsides and Downsides

"I almost want to say I'm a people person, but this term seems out of favor. I like the problem-solving part of design. Though I do aesthetically appealing things that look nice in the trade magazines, I get great satisfaction in organizing space to solve functional needs so people can work more effectively or live more comfortably. In real life, this is a team effort, as they say, which means that a lot can be compromised along the way because of lack of time, money, skill, desire, or plain bad taste.

"The building process is fraught with difficulty. People often joke that the best projects are those that remain in the flat file, that is, never get built. These are the ones where we can be sure of not having any problems in the field during construction. The profession is tough and often frustrating. Sometimes, I think that the ideal time to have been an architect was a century or so ago when, to oversimplify, I imagine they were predominantly upper-class, independently wealthy individuals who could design little projects for friends and family without having to worry about making money in the process.

"When you work on your own, you have much more control over what you are doing and you can do it as well as you can. As your practice grows, you can do more, but the downside is you must delegate responsibility to others and thereby lose control over what you loved doing in the first place. You cease being a designer and become a manager instead. This is the classic existential dilemma."

Advice from Harvey Schorr

"We have to chart our own course and make the most of the opportunities presented to us. I don't think a career path has a cookbook approach, nor can all the will in the world make someone into what he or she is not. One could study Frank Lloyd Wright, or anyone else, for a lifetime and never be able to comprehend or replicate how he did what he did. Many paths exist to truth, and one can play many potentially satisfying roles as an architect or as a member of the allied professions. I would include in this everything from weekend carpentry to government service to real estate development.

"I think the outlook is positive, subject to the lack of stability alluded to earlier. Pay is an issue to some degree: architects are not particularly well paid, at least in comparison to other professions (doctors, dentists, lawyers, accountants). Admittedly, we are not always focused on pay, and we find other avenues of fulfillment and job satisfaction besides money."

David DeCicco, Architect

David DiCicco is a self-employed architect in Taos, New Mexico. He's involved in residential, commercial, industrial, and institutional architecture and community and regional planning. He earned his B.Arch. in 1974 and his Master of Community and Regional Planning (M.S.R.P.) in 1988, both from North Dakota State University in Fargo. He has been working in the field since 1974.

Getting Started

"I did not intend to go to college immediately after high school, but the Vietnam war changed my mind. When I was there, the only curriculum that interested me was architecture. This was the field I knew the most about since my father and older brother were architects.

"While attending college, I was a janitor for several buildings, one of which was an architect/engineer's office. I convinced the person in charge to give me a job with their surveying department and worked my way into a project designer position in the architecture department. More recently, I held a position as the Taos County Planning Director, but a new election brought a commission that decided to replace those in office with people favored by the new government. I wanted to stay in Taos, and since I knew many people in the community, I decided to open a planning and architecture practice here in the fall of 1999."

What the Work Is Like

"As a sole proprietor and the only employee, I do everything from establishing client contacts to cleaning the office. Designing buildings and planning communities is incredibly rewarding, but designing a building is the beginning of what I do. I have to communicate that design to the builders in a way that will ensure that the client gets the building the architect designed and the building the client paid for.

"Some architects think that producing construction contract documents or working drawings is boring. I look for the creative aspects of work at every level, even drawing a window detail. I think an architect's design is only as good as the construction details the architect produces to complete the design.

"My typical day starts with an organizational period during which I plan the day and set out goals for what I want to accomplish by a certain time. For example, today, I have to produce three tenant plans for an industrial building that requires a large-scale floor plan, elevation, and sections of the construction. I have to plot them on a large-format printer, have them reproduced at a local print shop, and mail them to the client in Boston. I have a client meeting on a new project at 1:30 and a zoning board hearing for a client at 5:30. I have to check my account books and keep detailed records of how I spend my time so I can bill my clients fairly. By the time I get home tonight, I will have worked between ten to twelve hours. Though the day sounds hectic, it is busy, yet rewarding. I can see results at day's end.

"During my busy times I work between fifty to sixty hours per week. This is not always the case. If it were, I would be doing something different.

There are times when I have little or no work and spend my time marketing. I've had entire months with no work and then had months where I needed to complete two months' work in one. So it varies and is, therefore, never boring."

Upsides and Downsides

"I like that I am my own boss. I set my schedule, determine what work I will take, and help the community as much as possible. I enjoy my pro bono planning work with community organizations in Taos County, and I enjoy seeing a project that started as a vague discussion with the client come to fruition. One of the best parts of the profession is getting to meet and learn about how other people live and work. The downside is that if you are the kind of person who can't say no, you will, like me, end up working seven days per week."

Advice from David DiCicco

"Architects should be patient and have excellent people skills. You should develop and keep evolving a philosophical connection between your everyday life and your profession. Look at the world around you and see how you can help through community service that uses your profession to make life better for everyone. Most important, understand the consequences of whatever you do as a professional and a person.

"The job outlook is great, especially if you are willing to apply your architectural training to other fields such as planning, interior design, or product design."

George Hallowell, Architect

George Hallowell is vice president of Studio Pacifica, Ltd., an architecture and interior design firm in Seattle, Washington. He and his partner started the firm in 1993. His work involves a mixture of commercial and residential architecture, specializing in acoustically sensitive spaces such as recording studios and home theaters. He earned his B.A. in urban geography (urban planning) from the University of Washington in Seattle, and his Master's of Architecture from the University of Houston in Texas. He has been working in the field since 1983.

Getting Started

"As long as I can remember, certainly since childhood, I have been interested in architecture and building. I have an early memory of carrying my father's old briefcase around the house with 'architect' handwritten and taped on the side. As I grew up, I was always building and designing forts and tree houses.

"When I first went to college in 1971, I was registered in the undergraduate architecture program. But because of my age and the period in this country's history, I was a bit too rebellious to go along with all the requirements that the architecture program in my university put on incoming freshman. We were required to take a two-year series of support classes prior to being able to attend any architecture studio classes (the fun stuff). After complying with the requirements for various engineering and math classes, I realized that if the college thought that these support classes were what was important about architecture, I was not interested in the program. I graduated in Urban Geography, a sort of multidisciplinary urban planning program.

"After a series of jobs, including the design, construction, and operation of a recording studio, I decided I was still interested in architecture. I went back to graduate school in architecture in the early 1980s and have not looked back. My first job in architecture was as an intern in a small architectural design firm. I discovered the job through friends in the university and worked at that firm during the three years of the master's program.

"Most states require a period of internship before a person may take a licensing exam and become eligible for architectural licensing. In Texas, that period was three years. At the end of the internship is a four-day-long licensing exam. During the internship years, I was employed by a licensed architect and received specific components and areas of training. I was a recording engineer for about seven years in a recording studio in New Orleans, Louisiana, in the late 1970s. That training has allowed our firm to specialize in acoustically sensitive space design.

"One of my fellow students in the graduate architecture program and I had often dreamed of opening our own architecture firm someday. After we graduated, worked as interns for a number of years, and became licensed as architects, we decided to follow through on that dream."

What the Work Is Like

"As an owner of a small architecture firm, my duties are somewhat different from an architect who works for someone else's firm. A small firm changes what is required of the architect. Everything that goes on in our firm must be done by one of the three of us, so we each have to wear several hats. The only exception to this statement is accounting, which is done by our bookkeeper.

"I work on all the projects that come into the office. Because we tend to specialize in acoustic design or accessibility, my work is usually involved in residential or commercial recording studios, home theaters, film rooms, audio or video facilities, accessibility renovations, or new universal design (architectural design for people with differing physical needs). We work on projects that are altered or built new for wheelchair users (and other mobility devices), sight- or hearing-impaired users, and for people who are not able to use stairs or other physical barriers.

"When we design, one of the three of us usually assumes more of a lead role depending on the project. If the project is acoustical, I usually make first contact with the client and begin the information-gathering process. The client often comes to our office for the first meeting and discusses all of his or her project wants and needs. If the project is a new recording studio, we discuss how many rooms the client wants, the equipment the client uses, the acoustical parameters he or she wants us to follow, the look and feel of the building, the number and types of people that will use the building, and all of the other issues that will affect the design.

"The next step usually involves a design session with just the three of us. We sit down and begin to sketch the building's layout. We think about sight lines (seeing from room to room), ergonomics, movement of people through the spaces, sizes for equipment, light, and the feel and sound of the rooms. When we have one or more floor plan ideas for how the building might work, we meet again with the client. We think about how the building works in three dimensions. Do the rooms have high ceilings, are the ceilings flat or sloped, what will the rooms feel like, and so on. If the project were a house instead of a recording studio, we would think about how the house looks from the outside: its height, how is it massed, and how it sits on the site.

"We have to research building codes and other legal requirements of the municipality and state. When we have some ideas for the three-dimensional design of the building, we usually meet again with the client. Somewhere in this step, we begin to put the design in computer-aided design (CAD). Except for the early sketching process, most of our work is done on the computer. Our office only has one small drafting table, and we almost never use it.

"We can design a project for a client, but we need to get the client. In our firm, we are involved in the marketing process. Marketing duties include going out to meet prospective clients, sending letters and e-mails, creating advertisements, writing magazine or newspaper articles, applying for awards, creating job sheets (individual handout sheets describing projects we have designed), responding to requests for information, and creating and managing our website.

"Keeping a small architecture firm running requires filing, typing, copying, sorting, bookkeeping, hiring and firing, and managing a library of construction materials and information. It requires keeping our computer system running properly. Though some of these tasks could be done by outside people or services, we do them ourselves.

"My day is usually from 9:00 a.m. to 6:00 p.m. with an hour for lunch. We usually have ten to twenty-five jobs active at any given time. In other offices I have worked in, the hours and pace of the job can be different. When I worked in New York City, for example, I sometimes worked more overtime than regular time: eighty to ninety hours a week."

Upsides and Downsides

"I like the design portion of the job. I most enjoy creating a floor plan or a building shape and seeing it come to life in a built project. There is nothing quite like walking through a space that came out of your imagination. But I don't enjoy the hassle over time schedules or payment that is a part of the operation of any small business."

Advice from George Hallowell

"A career in architecture comes from a love of the profession. Most architects did not go into the profession to make a huge salary or get an easy job; they just enjoy the creation process. I don't think that most successful architects were born with some innate talent, but they put in the effort and time to hone their skills.

"Architects often come from many backgrounds, from astronomy to zoology, before getting their architectural degree. I found drafting classes in high school useful. I have enjoyed classes and independent study courses in art and history. I had part-time jobs in the construction industry (as a carpenter) to learn the trade. These jobs helped me understand the components and systems that go into buildings, but I know many architects who did not follow this process and are successful.

"An overall life experience and that spark of joy in the creation of a new space or form is the key to success. Investigate buildings you like, talk to people in the profession, look into good architecture education programs, and read some of the many good books on the profession.

"The job outlook for young architects in this part of the country is good now. Most firms are on the hunt for good people. Architecture, as with any business, is part of the larger economic cycle, however. As new construction is reduced, so are the jobs for architects."

PROFESSIONAL ASSOCIATIONS

ARCHITECTURE

American Institute of Architects (AIA)
1735 New York Ave. NW
Washington, DC 20006
aia.org

The American Institute of Architects (AIA) represents the architectural profession and provides resources and tools to its more than 66,000 members. The AIA has twenty-two professional interest areas such as healthcare facilities, the environment, historic resources, interiors, housing, educational facilities, building codes and standards, and international practice.

For information about education and careers in architecture, consult the AIA Career Center.

Association of Collegiate Schools of Architecture (ACAS)
1735 New York Ave. NW
Washington, DC 20006
acsa-arch.org

National Architectural Accrediting Board (NAAB)
1735 New York Ave. NW
Washington, DC 20006
naab.org

The NAAB, established in 1940, is the sole agency authorized to accredit U.S. professional degrees in architecture.

Society of American Registered Architects
14 E. 38th St., Eleventh Floor
New York, NY 10016
sara-national.org

National Council of Architectural Registration Boards (NCARB)
1801 K St. NW, Suite 700-K
Washington, DC 20006
ncarb.org
For more information about registration and internship, write to your state registration board *or* contact the National Council of Architectural Registration Boards.

The Intern Development Program (IDP) information package can be requested from NCARB. Or contact your local American Institute of Architects (AIA) chapter or AIA headquarters.

NCARB Intern-Architect Development Program
1801 K St. NW, Suite 1100
Washington, DC 20006
ncarb.org/idp

CONSTRUCTION

For information about career opportunities, certification, and educational programs in cost estimating in the construction industry, consult the following sources:

Association for the Advancement of Cost Engineering International (AACEI)
209 Prairie Ave., Suite 100
Morgantown, WV 26501
aacei.org

Professional Construction Estimators Association of America
P.O. Box 11626
Charlotte, NC 28220
rea.com/careers/estimators.cfm

For similar information about cost estimating in government, manufacturing, and other industries, consult the following source:

Society of Cost Estimating and Analysis
527 Maple Ave. E., Suite 301
Vienna, VA 22180
sceaonline.net

For information about career opportunities in the construction industry, consult the following sources:

Associated Builders and Contractors (ABC)
4250 N. Fairfax Dr., Ninth Floor
Arlington, VA 22203
abc.org

Associated General Contractors of America
2300 Wilson Blvd., Suite 400
Arlington, VA 22201
agc.org

For information about constructor certification and professional career opportunities in the construction industry, consult the following source:

American Institute of Constructors
P.O. Box 26334
Alexandria, VA 22314
aicnet.org

For information about construction management and construction manager certification, consult the following source:

Construction Management Association of America
7926 Jones Branch Dr., Suite 800
McLean, VA 22102
cmaanet.org

For information on accredited construction science and management programs and accreditation requirements, consult the following source:

American Council for Construction Education
1717 N. Loop 1604 E., Suite 320
San Antonio, TX 78232
acce-hq.org

ENGINEERING

For college students interested in obtaining information on professional engineer licensure, consult the following source:

The National Society of Professional Engineers
1420 King St.
Alexandria, VA 22314
nspe.org

For those seeking employment with the U.S. government, consult the following source:

usajobs.opm.gov

For high school students interested in obtaining information on ABET-accredited engineering programs, consult the following source:

Accreditation Board for Engineering and Technology
111 Market Place, Suite 1050
Baltimore, MD 21202
abet.org

For high school students interested in obtaining general information on various engineering disciplines, contact the Junior Engineering Technical Society by sending a business-size SASE (with six first-class stamps affixed) to the following address:

JETS-Guidance
1420 King St., Suite 405
Alexandria, VA 22314
jets.org

For information on the various fields of engineering, consult the following sources:

American Society of Civil Engineers
1801 Alexander Bell Dr.
Reston, VA 20191
asce.org

American Society of Heating, Refrigerating, and Air-Conditioning Engineers
1791 Tullie Cir. NE
Atlanta, GA 30329
ashrae.org

American Society of Mechanical Engineers International
Three Park Ave.
New York, NY 10016
asme.org

Institute of Electrical and Electronics Engineers
1828 L St. NW, Suite 1202
Washington, DC 20036
ieee.org

The Minerals, Metals, and Materials Society
184 Thorn Hill Rd.
Warrendale, PA 15086
tms.org

National Society of Professional Engineers
1420 King St.
Alexandria, VA 22314
nspe.org

HISTORIC PRESERVATION

Advisory Council on Historic Preservation
1100 Pennsylvania Ave. NW, Suite 803
Old Post Office Building
Washington, DC 20004
achp.gov

Association for Preservation Technology International
3085 Stevenson Dr., Suite 200
Springfield, IL 62703
apti.org

National Register of Historic Places
National Park Service
1201 Eye St. NW, Eighth Floor (MS 2280)
Washington, DC 20005
cr.nps.gov/nr

National Trust for Historic Preservation
1785 Massachusetts Ave. NW
Washington, DC 20036
nthp.org

Society of Architectural Historians
1365 N. Astor
Chicago, IL 60610
sah.org

LANDSCAPE ARCHITECTURE

For general information on registration or licensing requirements for landscape architects in the United States and Canada, consult the following two sources:

Bureau of Land Management
U.S. Department of the Interior
Office of Public Affairs
1849 C St., Room 406-LS
Washington, DC 20240
blm.gov

Canadian Society of Landscape Architects
P.O. Box 13594
Ottawa, ON K2K 1XS
Canada
csla.ca

The following sources also offer further information on landscape architecture and related fields.

American Forests
910 Seventeenth St. NW, Suite 600
Washington, DC 20006
americanforests.org

American Nursery and Landscape Association
1000 Vermont Ave. NW, Suite 300
Washington, DC 20005
anla.org

American Society of Consulting Arborists
15245 Shady Grove Rd., Suite 130
Rockville, MD 20850
asca-consultants.org

American Society of Landscape Architects
636 Eye St. NW
Washington, DC 20001
asla.org

Associated Landscape Contractors of America
150 Elden St., Suite 270
Herndon, VA 20170
alca.org

Association of Professional Landscape Designers
4305 N. Sixth St., Suite A
Harrisburg PA, 17110
apld.org

Colonial Williamsburg Foundation
P.O. Box 1776
Williamsburg, VA 23187
history.org

Council of Educators in Landscape Architecture
P.O. Box 7506
Edmond, OK 73083
thecela.org

Council of Landscape Architectural Registration Boards
3949 Pender Dr., Suite 120
Fairfax, VA 22030
clarb.org

Golf Course Superintendents Association of America
1421 Research Park Dr.
Lawrence, KS 66049
gcsaa.org

National Park Service
U.S. Department of the Interior
1849 C St. NW
Washington, DC 20240
nps.gov

National Pest Management Association
9300 Lee Highway, Suite 301
Fairfax, VA 22031
pestworld.org

National Wildlife Federation
11100 Wildlife Center Dr.
Reston, VA 20190
nwf.org

Professional Grounds Management Society
720 Light St.
Baltimore, MD 21230
pgms.org

Society of American Foresters
5400 Grosvenor Ln.
Bethesda, MD 20814
safnet.org

Student Conservation Association
689 River Rd./P.O. Box 550
Charlestown, NH 03603
thesca.org

U.S.D.A. Forest Service
1400 Independence Ave. SW
Washington, DC 20250
fs.fed.us

World Forestry Center
4033 S.W. Canyon Rd.
Portland, OR 97221
worldforestry.org

MONUMENTS

International Council on Monuments and Sites
49–51, rue de la Fédération
75015 Paris
France
icomos.org/ICOMOS_Main_Page.html
ICOMOS is an international, nongovernmental organization dedicated to the conservation of the world's historic monuments and sites. The organization was founded in 1965 as a result of the international adoption of the Charter for the Conservation and Restoration of Monuments and Sites in Venice the year before. Today, the organization has national committees in over ninety countries.

US/ICOMOS
National Building Museum
401 F St. NW, Suite 331
Washington, DC 20001
nbm.org
icomos.org/usicomos
This is the national committee of the International Council on Monuments and Sites for the United States.

TERRA COTTA

Friends of Terra Cotta
c/o Tunick
771 W. End Ave. #10E
New York, NY 10025
preserve.org/fotc

The Friends of Terra Cotta, a national nonprofit organization, was founded to promote education and research in the preservation of architectural terra cotta and related ceramic materials. The organization seeks to educate the general public and construction industry professionals about architectural terra cotta's value and history as a building material.

URBAN PLANNING

For information on careers, salaries, and certification in urban and regional planning, consult the following source:

American Planning Association, Education Division
122 S. Michigan Ave., Suite 1600
Chicago, IL 60603
planning.org

ADDITIONAL ASSOCIATIONS AND WEBSITES

American Concrete Institute
38800 Country Club Dr.
Farmington Hills, MI 48331
concrete.org

American Council of Engineering Companies
1015 Fifteenth St. NW, Eighth Floor
Washington, DC 20005
acec.org

American Public Gardens Association
100 W. Tenth St., Suite 614
Wilmington, DE 19801
publicgardens.org

American Society of Golf Course Architects
125 N. Executive Dr., Suite 106
Brookfield, WI 53005
asgca.org

American Society of Interior Designers
608 Massachusetts Ave. NE
Washington, DC 20002
asid.org

American Subcontractors Association
1004 Duke St.
Alexandria, VA 22314
asaonline.com

Architecture Research Institute
20 River Terrace at Lexington Ave.
New York, NY 10001
architect.org

Canadian Center for Architecture
1920 Baile St.
Montreal, QC H3H 2S6
Canada
cca.qc.ca

Canadian Masonry Research Institute
10712–176 St., Suite 200
Edmonton, AB T5S G57
Canada

Center for Health Design
1850 Gateway Blvd., Suite 1083
Concord, CA 94520
healthdesign.org

Center for Resourceful Building Technology
P.O. Box 100
Missoula, MT 59806
crbtdb.ncat.org

Construction Industry Computing Association
Oxford House
Oxford Rd.
Manchester M1 7Ed
England
cica.org.uk

Construction Industry Research and Information Association
Classic House
174–180 Old St.
London EC1V 98P
England
ciria.org.uk

Construction Innovation Forum
6494 Latcha Rd.
Walbridge, OH 43465
cif.org

Construction Management Association of America
7926 Jones Branch Dr., Suite 800
McLean, VA 22102
cmaanet.org

Construction Specifications Institute
99 Canal Center Plaza, Suite 300
Alexandria, VA 22314
csinet.org

Council of Planning Librarians
1408 W. Gregory Dr.
Urbana, IL 61801
library.uiuc.edu

Council on Tall Buildings and Urban Habitat
Illinois Institute of Technology
S.R. Crown Hall
3360 S. State St.
Chicago, IL 60616
ctbuh.org

Design Management Institute
101 Tremont St., Suite 300
Boston, MA 02108
dmi.org

Exhibit Designers and Producers Association
1100 Johnson Ferry Rd., Suite 300
Atlanta, GA 30342
edpa.com

Frank Lloyd Wright Foundation, Taliesin West
P.O. Box 4430
Scottsdale, AZ 85261
franklloydwright.org

Frank Lloyd Wright Home and Studio Foundation
931 Chicago Ave.
Oak Park, IL 60302
wrightplus.org

Furniture History Society
1 Mercedes Cottages
St. John's Rd., Hayward's Heath
West Sussex RH16 4EH
England
furniturehistorysociety.org

Green Building Council
110 Sutter St., Suite 410
San Francisco, CA 94104
usgbc.org

Healthy House Institute
13998 W. Hartford Dr.
Boise, ID 83713
hhinst.com

Historic American Buildings Survey
National Park Service
1201 Eye St. NW, Eighth Floor (MS 2280)
Washington, DC 20005
cr.nps.gov/nr

Illuminating Engineering Society of North America
120 Wall St., Seventeenth Floor
New York, NY 10005
iesna.org

Industrial Designers Society of America
1142 Walker Rd.
Great Falls, VA 22066
idsa.org

Industrial Fabrics Association International
1801 County Rd. B W
Roseville, MN 55113
ifai.com

Institute of Store Planners
25 N. Broadway
Tarrytown, NY 10590
ispo.org

Institute of Urban and Regional Development
University of California
316 Wurster Hall #1870
Berkeley, CA 94720
www-iurd.ced.berkeley.edu

International Association of Lighting Designers
The Merchandise Mart, Suite 9–104
Chicago, IL 60654
iald.org

International Association of Plumbing and Mechanical Officials
20001 E. Walnut Dr. S.
Walnut, CA 91789
iapmo.org

International Building Performance Simulation Association
Member Services Officer, Energy Systems Laboratory
Department of Architecture
Texas A&M University System
College Station, TX 77843
ibpsa.org

International Code Council
5203 Leesburg Pike, Suite 600
Falls Church, VA 22041
intlcode.org

International Council on Monuments and Sites
International Facility Management Association
1 E. Greenway Plaza, Suite 1100
Houston, TX 77046
ifma.org

International Federation for Housing and Planning
Secretariat
Wassenaarseweg 43
2596 CG The Hague
The Netherlands
ifhp.org

International Interior Design Association
222 Merchandise Mart, Suite 567
Chicago, IL 60654
iida.org

Landscape Design Trust
Bank Chambers
1 London Rd.
Redhill, Surrey RH1 1LY
England
landscape.co.uk

Landscape Institute (UK)
33 Great Portland St.
London W1W 8QG
England
landscapeinstitute.org

National Association of Environmental Professionals
389 Main St., Suite 202
Malden, MA 02148
naep.org

National Association of Home Builders
1201 Fifteenth St. NW
Washington, DC 20005
nahb.com

National Association of Home Builders Research Center
400 Prince George's Blvd.
Upper Marlboro, MD 20774
nahbrc.org

National Association of Housing and Redevelopment Officials
630 Eye St. NW
Washington, DC 20001
nahro.org

National Association of Industrial and Office Properties
2201 Cooperative Way, Third Floor
Herndon, VA 20171
naiop.org

National Building Museum
401 F St. NW
Washington, DC 20001
nbm.org

National Organization of Minority Architects
c/o School of Architecture and Design
College of Engineering, Architecture, and Computer Science
Howard University
2366 Sixth St. NW, Room 100
Washington, DC 20059
noma.net

National Recreation and Park Association
22377 Belmont Ridge Rd.
Ashburn, VA 20148
nrpa.org

National Renewable Energy Laboratory
1617 Cole Blvd.
Golden, CO 80401
nrel.gov

National Research Council of Canada
Institute for Research in Construction
Ottawa, ON K1A 0R6
Canada
nrc.ca/irc

Organization of Black Designers
300 M St. SW, Suite N110
Washington, DC 20024
core77.com/OBD

Partners for Livable Communities
1429 Twenty-first St. NW
Washington, DC 20036
livable.com

Partners for Sacred Places
1700 Sansom St., Tenth Floor
Philadelphia, PA 19103
sacredplaces.org

Planners Network
c/o Pratt GCPE
379 DeKalb Ave.
Brooklyn, NY 11205
plannersnetwork.org

Planning Advisory Service
122 S. Michigan Ave., Suite 1600
Chicago, IL 60603
planning.org/pas/pas.html

Plumbing Heating Cooling Contractors Association
180 S. Washington St.
P.O. Box 6808
Falls Church, VA 22040
naphcc.org

Rails to Trails Conservancy
1100 Seventeenth St. NW, Tenth Floor
Washington, DC 20036
railtrails.org

Regional Plan Association (NY, NJ, CT)
4 Irving Place, Seventh Floor
New York, NY 10003
rpa.org

Royal Institute of British Architects
66 Portland Place
London W1B 1AD
England
architecture.com

Society for Environmental Graphic Design
401 F St. NW, Suite 333
Washington, DC 20001
segd.org

Society of Architectural Historians of Great Britain
Pixham Mill, Pixham Lane
Dorking, Surrey RH14 1PQ
England
sahgb.org.uk/index.html

Solar Energy Industries Association Members Database
1616 H St. NW, Eighth Floor
Washington, DC 20006
seia.org/main.htm

Trust for Public Land
116 New Montgomery St., Fourth Floor
San Francisco, CA 94105
tpl.org

UIA International Union of Architects
51, Rue Raynouard
-75016 Paris
France
uia-architectes.org

Urban and Regional Information Systems Association
1460 Renaissance Dr., Suite 305
Park Ridge, IL 60068
urisa.org

Vernacular Architecture Forum
P.O. Box 1511
Harrisonburg, VA 22801
vernaculararchitecture.org/rframe.htm

Wallcoverings Association
401 N. Michigan Ave.
Chicago, IL 60611
wallcoverings.org

FURTHER READING

ARCHITECTURE PROGRAMS

Guide to Graduate Degree Programs in Architectural History, compiled by Richard Betts. Available through:

Society of Architectural Historians
1232 Pine St.
Philadelphia, PA 19107

Guide to Architecture Schools by the Association of Collegiate Schools of Architecture
The guide is available in most architecture libraries and bookstores and can be ordered directly from the Association of Collegiate Schools of Architecture (ACSA):

Association of Collegiate Schools of Architecture
1735 New York Ave. NW
Washington, DC 20006
acsa-arch.org

ARCHITECTURE SCHOOLS: SPECIAL PROGRAMS

The ACSA annually publishes a list of summer programs in Architecture Schools: Special Programs:

acsa-arch.org/store/guide.aspx

HISTORIC PRESERVATION

Historic Preservation magazine and *Historic Preservation News* are published by the National Trust for Historic Preservation (NTHP):

National Trust for Historic Preservation
1785 Massachusetts Ave. NW
Washington, DC 20036
preservationnation.org

Other publications available through the National Trust for Historic Preservation website include the following:

Challenging Sprawl: Organizational Responses to a National Problem
Getting Started: How to Succeed in Heritage Tourism
Heritage Resources Law: Protecting the Archeological and Cultural Environment
National Trust Guide to Historic Bed and Breakfasts, Inns, and Small Hotels
Preserving Our Past: Building Our Future

LANDSCAPE ARCHITECTURE

The following publications from the American Society of Landscape Architects are available through its website asla.org:

Landscape Architecture magazine (LAM)
Landscape Architecture News Digest (LAND)
Landscape Architecture Technical Information Series Online (LATIS Online)
ASLA Reports, Surveys, and Proceedings

ACCREDITED TRAINING PROGRAMS FOR ARCHITECTURE IN THE UNITED STATES, PUERTO RICO, AND CANADA

UNITED STATES

Alabama

Auburn University (B.Arch.)
College of Architecture, Design, and Construction
202 Dudley Commons
Auburn University, AL 36849
cadc.auburn.edu

Tuskegee University (B.Arch.)
Department of Architecture
School of Engineering, Architecture, and Physical Sciences
Tuskegee, AL 36088
tuskegee.edu/Global/category.asp?C=35304

Arizona

Arizona State University (M.Arch.)
School of Architecture
Tempe, AZ 85287
http://design.asu.edu/sala/index.shtml

Frank Lloyd Wright School of Architecture (M.Arch.)
Taliesin West
Scottsdale, AZ 85261
taliesin.edu

University of Arizona (B.Arch.)
College of Architecture, Planning, and Landscape
Tucson, AZ 85721
architecture.arizona.edu

Arkansas

University of Arkansas (B.Arch.)
School of Architecture
120 Vol Walker Hall
Fayetteville, AR 72701
http://architecture.uark.edu/

California

California Polytechnic State University, San Luis Obispo (B.Arch.)
College of Architecture and Environmental Design
San Luis Obispo, CA 93407
arch.calpoly.edu

California State Polytechnic University, Pomona (B.Arch., M.Arch.)
Department of Architecture
3801 W. Temple Ave.
Pomona, CA 91768
csupomona.edu

Southern California Institute of Architecture (B.Arch., M.Arch.)
5454 Beethoven St.
Los Angeles, CA 90066
sciarc.edu

University of California, Berkeley (M.Arch.)
Department of Architecture
232 Wurster Hall
Berkeley, CA 94720
arch.ced.berkeley.edu/

University of California, Los Angeles (M.Arch.)
Department of Architecture and Urban Design
1317 Perloff Hall
Los Angeles, CA 90095
aud.ucla.edu

University of Southern California (B.Arch.)
School of Architecture
Los Angeles, CA 90089
usc.edu/dept/architecture

Woodbury University (B.Arch.)
Department of Architecture
7500 Glenoaks Blvd.
Burbank, CA 91510
woodbury.edu

Colorado

University of Colorado at Denver/Boulder (M.Arch.)
College of Architecture and Planning
Campus Box 126
P.O. Box 173364
Denver, CO 80217
http://www.cudenver.edu/Academics/Colleges/ArchitecturePlanning/Pages/home.aspx

Connecticut

Yale University (M.Arch.)
School of Architecture
180 York St.
P.O. Box 208242
New Haven, CT 06520
architecture.yale.edu

District of Columbia

Catholic University of America (B.Arch., M.Arch.)
School of Architecture and Planning
620 Michigan Ave. NE
Washington, DC 20064
cua.edu/www/apu/index.htm

Howard University (B.Arch.)
School of Architecture and Design
2366 Sixth St. NW
Washington, DC 20059
howard.edu/ceacs/

Florida

Florida A&M University (B.Arch., M.Arch.)
School of Architecture
1936 S. Martin Luther King Jr. Blvd.
Tallahassee, FL 32307
famusoa.net/

Florida Atlantic University
777 Glades Rd.
P.O. Box 3091
Boca Raton, FL 33431
fau.edu/arch/

Florida International University
University Park Campus
11200 S.W. 8th St.
Miami, FL 33199
fiu.edu/~soa/

University of Florida (M.Arch.)
Department of Architecture
P.O. Box 115702
Gainesville, FL 32611
dcp.ufl.edu/arch/

University of Miami (B.Arch., M.Arch.)
School of Architecture
P.O. Box 249178
Coral Gables, FL 33124
arc.miami.edu

University of South Florida (M.Arch.)
School of Architecture and Community Design
3702 Spectrum Blvd., Suite 180
Tampa, FL 33612
arch.usf.edu

Georgia

Georgia Institute of Technology (M.Arch.)
College of Architecture
Atlanta, GA 30332
coa.gatech.edu/cgis/

Savannah College of Art and Design (B.Arch.)
Department of Architecture
201 W. Charlton St.
Savannah, GA 31401
scad.edu

Southern Polytechnic State University (B.Arch.)
School of Architecture
1100 S. Marietta Parkway
Marietta, GA 30060
spsu.edu/home/academics/architecture.html

Hawaii

University of Hawaii at Manoa (B.Arch., M.Arch.)
School of Architecture
2410 Campus Rd.
Honolulu, HI 96822
arch.hawaii.edu/site/index.php

Idaho

University of Idaho (B.Arch.)
Department of Architecture
Moscow, ID 83844
caa.uidaho.edu/arch/

Illinois

Illinois Institute of Technology (B.Arch., M.Arch.)
College of Architecture, S. R. Crown Hall
3360 S. State St.
Chicago, IL 60616
iit.edu/arch/

University of Illinois at Chicago (B.Arch., M.Arch.)
School of Architecture
845 W. Harrison St., M/C 030
Chicago, IL 60607
arch.uic.edu/index.php

University of Illinois at Urbana-Champaign (M.Arch.)
School of Architecture
Temple Hoyne Buell Hall
611 Taft Dr.
Champaign, IL 61820
arch.uiuc.edu/

Indiana

Ball State University (B.Arch.)
College of Architecture and Planning
Muncie, IN 47306
bsu.edu/cap

University of Notre Dame (B.Arch., M.Arch.)
School of Architecture
110 Bond Hall
Notre Dame, IN 46556
http://architecture.nd.edu/

Iowa

Iowa State University (B.Arch., M.Arch.)
Department of Architecture
156 College of Design
Ames, IA 50011
wwdesign.iastate.edu/ARCH/

Kansas

Kansas State University (B.Arch.)
Department of Architecture
College of Architecture, Planning, and Design
Manhattan, KS 66506
http://capd.ksu.edu/

University of Kansas (B.Arch., M.Arch.)
School of Architecture and Urban Design
Lawrence, KS 66045
saud.ku.edu/

Kentucky

University of Kentucky (B.Arch.)
College of Architecture, Pence Hall
Lexington, KY 40506
uky.edu/Design/

Louisiana

Louisiana State University (B.Arch.)
School of Architecture, College of Design
136 Atkinson Hall
Baton Rouge, LA 70803
http://design.lsu.edu/architecture.htm

Louisiana Tech University (B.Arch.)
School of Architecture
P.O. Box 3147
Ruston, LA 71272
latech.edu/tech/liberal-arts/architecture/SOAhome.htm

Southern University and A&M College (B.Arch.)
School of Architecture
Baton Rouge, LA 70813
http://susa.subr.edu/

Tulane University (B.Arch., M.Arch.)
School of Architecture, Richardson Memorial Hall
New Orleans, LA 70118
http://architecture.tulane.edu/home/

University of Louisiana at Lafayette (formerly University of Southwestern Louisiana) (B.Arch.)
School of Architecture
Lafayette, LA 70504
http://arts.louisiana.edu/

Maryland

Morgan State University (M.Arch.)
Institute of Architecture and Planning
Baltimore, MD 21239
morgan.edu/academics/IAP/bsae_home.html

University of Maryland (M.Arch.)
School of Architecture
College Park, MD 20742
arch.umd.edu/

Massachusetts

Boston Architectural Center (B.Arch.)
320 Newbury St.
Boston, MA 02115
the-bac.edu

Harvard University (M.Arch.)
Department of Architecture
48 Quincy St.
Cambridge, MA 02138
gsd.harvard.edu

Massachusetts Institute of Technology (M.Arch.)
Department of Architecture
77 Massachusetts Ave.
Cambridge, MA 02139
sap.mit.edu

Wentworth Institute of Technology (B.Arch.)
Department of Architecture
550 Huntington Ave.
Boston, MA 02115
wit.edu

Michigan

Andrews University (B.Arch.)
Division of Architecture
Berrien Springs, MI 49104
andrews.edu/arch/

Lawrence Technological University (M.Arch.)
College of Architecture and Design
21000 W. Ten Mile Rd.
Southfield, MI 48075
ltu.edu/architecture_and_design/index.asp

University of Detroit, Mercy (B.Arch.)
School of Architecture
P.O. Box 19900
Detroit, MI 48219
http://architecture.udmercy.edu/

University of Michigan (M.Arch.)
College of Architecture and Urban Planning
Ann Arbor, MI 48109
tcaup.umich.edu/

Minnesota

University of Minnesota (M.Arch.)
Department of Architecture
89 Church St. SE
Minneapolis, MN 55455
http://arch.design.umn.edu/

Mississippi

Mississippi State University (B.Arch., M.Arch.)
School of Architecture
College of Architecture, Art, and Design
32 Giles Hall
Mississippi State, MS 39762
www.grad.coa.msstate.edu/program_overview.htm

Missouri

Drury College (B.Arch.)
Hammons School of Architecture
Springfield, MO 65802
drury.edu/section/section.cfm?sid=48

Washington University (M.Arch.)
School of Architecture
One Brookings Dr.
St. Louis, MO 63130
arch.wustl.edu/

Montana

Montana State University (B.Arch., M.Arch.)
School of Architecture
Bozeman, MT 59717
arch.montana.edu/

Nebraska

University of Nebraska (M.Arch.)
College of Architecture
210 Architecture Hall
Lincoln, NE 68588
http://archweb.unl.edu/

Nevada

University of Nevada, Las Vegas (M.Arch.)
School of Architecture
4505 Maryland Parkway
Las Vegas, NV 89154
http://architecture.unlv.edu/

New Jersey

New Jersey Institute of Technology (M.Arch.)
School of Architecture, University Heights
Newark, NJ 07102
http://architecture.njit.edu/

Princeton University (M.Arch.)
School of Architecture
Princeton, NJ 08544
soa.princeton.edu/

New Mexico

University of New Mexico (M.Arch.)
School of Architecture and Planning
2414 Central Southeast
Albuquerque, NM 87131
saap.unm.edu/

New York

City College of the City University of New York (B.Arch.)
School of Architecture, Urban Design, and Landscape Architecture
138th St. at Convent Ave., Shepard Hall 103
New York, NY 10031
www1.ccny.cuny.edu/prospective/architecture

Columbia University (M.Arch.)
Graduate School of Architecture, Planning, and Preservation
New York, NY 10027
arch.columbia.edu/

Cooper Union (B.Arch.)
The Irwin S. Chanin School of Architecture
Cooper Square
New York, NY 10003
http://archweb.cooper.edu/

Cornell University (B.Arch.)
Department of Architecture
143 E. Sibley
Ithaca, NY 14853
http://aap.cornell.edu/

New York Institute of Technology (B.Arch.)
School of Architecture and Design
Old Westbury, NY 11568
nyit.edu

Parsons School of Design (M.Arch.)
Department of Architecture
66 Fifth Ave.
New York, NY 10011
http://www2.parsons.edu/architecture/news.htm

Pratt Institute (B.Arch.)
School of Architecture
200 Willoughby Ave.
Brooklyn, NY 11205
pratt.edu/school_of_architecture

Rensselaer Polytechnic Institute (B.Arch., M.Arch.)
School of Architecture
110 Eighth St.
Troy, NY 12180
arch.rpi.edu/

State University of New York at Buffalo (M.Arch.)
School of Architecture and Planning
112 Hayes Hall
3435 Main St.
Buffalo, NY 14214
www.ap.buffalo.edu/

Syracuse University (B.Arch., M.Arch.)
School of Architecture
103 Slocum Hall
Syracuse, NY 13244
http://soa.syr.edu/index.php

North Carolina

North Carolina State University (B.Arch., M.Arch.)
Department of Architecture
Box 7701
Raleigh, NC 27695
ncsu.edu/design

University of North Carolina at Charlotte (B.Arch.)
College of Architecture
Charlotte, NC 28223
www.coa.uncc.edu/

North Dakota

North Dakota State University (B.Arch.)
Department of Architecture and Landscape Architecture
SU Station, P.O. Box 5285
Fargo, ND 58105
http://ala.ndsu.edu/

Ohio

Kent State University (B.Arch.)
School of Architecture and Environmental Design
200 Taylor Hall
Kent, OH 44242
www.caed.kent.edu/

Miami University (M.Arch.)
Department of Architecture
101 Alumni Hall
Oxford, OH 45056
muohio.edu

Ohio State University (M.Arch.)
Austin E. Knowlton School of Architecture
Columbus, OH 43210
http://knowlton.osu.edu/

University of Cincinnati (B.Arch.)
School of Architecture and Interior Design
Cincinnati, OH 45221
http://daap.uc.edu/

Oklahoma

Oklahoma State University (B.Arch.)
School of Architecture
Stillwater, OK 74078
http://architecture.ceat.okstate.edu/

University of Oklahoma (B.Arch., M.Arch.)
College of Architecture
830 Van Vleet Oval
Norman, OK 73019
http://coa.ou.edu/

Oregon

University of Oregon (B.Arch., M.Arch.)
Department of Architecture
210 Lawrence Hall
1206 University of Oregon
Eugene, OR 97403
http://architecture.uoregon.edu/
The accredited M.Arch. program is offered on the Eugene and Portland campuses.

Pennsylvania

Carnegie Mellon University (B.Arch.)
School of Architecture
201 College of Fine Arts
Pittsburgh, PA 15213
www.arc.cmu.edu/cmu/index.jsp

Drexel University (B.Arch.)
Department of Architecture
Philadelphia, PA 19104
drexel.edu/westphal/academics/undergraduate/architecture/

Pennsylvania State University (B.Arch.)
Department of Architecture
College of Arts and Architecture
206 Engineering Unit C
University Park, PA 16802
www.arch.psu.edu

Philadelphia University (formerly
Philadelphia College of Textiles and Science) (B.Arch.)
School of Architecture and Design
School House Ln. and Henry Ave.
Philadelphia, PA 19144
www.philau.edu/architecture

Temple University (B.Arch.)
Architecture Program
Twelfth and Norris St.
Philadelphia, PA 19122
www.temple.edu/architecture

University of Pennsylvania (M.Arch.)
Department of Architecture
207 Meyerson Hall
Philadelphia, PA 19104
www.design.upenn.edu/new/arch/index.php

Puerto Rico

University of Puerto Rico (M.Arch.)
School of Architecture
P.O. Box 21909
San Juan, PR 00931

Rhode Island

Rhode Island School of Design (B.Arch., M.Arch.)
Department of Architecture
2 College St.
Providence, RI 02903
www.risd.edu

Roger Williams University (B.Arch.)
School of Architecture
One Old Ferry Rd.
Briston, RI 02809
rwu.edu/academics/schools/saahp

South Carolina

Clemson University (M.Arch.)
College of Architecture, Arts, and Humanities
School of Architecture
Clemson, SC 29634
clemson.edu/caah

Tennessee

University of Tennessee, Knoxville (B.Arch., M.Arch.)
College of Architecture and Planning
Knoxville, TN 37996
www.arch.utk.edu

Texas

Prairie View A&M University (B.Arch.)
Division of Architecture
P.O. Box 397
Prairie View, TX 77446
pvamu.edu

Rice University (B.Arch., M.Arch.)
School of Architecture
6100 Main St., MS #50
Houston, TX 77005
arch.rice.edu

Texas A&M University (M.Arch.)
Department of Architecture
College Station, TX 77843
http://archone.tamu.edu/College

Texas Tech University (B.Arch., M.Arch.)
College of Architecture
P.O. Box 42091
Lubbock, TX 79409
www.ttu.edu/colleges/arch.php

University of Houston (B.Arch., M.Arch.)
Gerald D. Hines College of Architecture
Houston, TX 77204
www.arch.uh.edu

University of Texas at Arlington (M.Arch.)
School of Architecture
Box 19108
Arlington, TX 76019
www.uta.edu/architecture

University of Texas at Austin (B.Arch., M.Arch.)
School of Architecture
1 University Station B7500
Austin, TX 78712
http://soa.utexas.edu/

Utah

University of Utah (M.Arch.)
Graduate School of Architecture
375 S. 1530 E. Room 235
Salt Lake City, UT 84112
arch.utah.edu

Vermont

Norwich University (B.Arch.)
Division of Architecture and Art
Northfield, VT 05663
norwich.edu

Virginia

Hampton University (B.Arch.)
Department of Architecture
Hampton, VA 23668
www.hamptonu.edu

University of Virginia (M.Arch.)
School of Architecture
Campbell Hall
Charlottesville, VA 22903
virginia.edu

Virginia Polytechnic Institute and State University (B.Arch., M.Arch.)
College of Architecture and Urban Studies
Blacksburg, VA 24061
www.arch.vt.edu

Washington

University of Washington (M.Arch.)
Department of Architecture
Box 355720
Seattle, WA 98195
http://depts.washington.edu/archdept/

Washington State University (B.Arch.)
School of Architecture
P.O. Box 642220
Pullman, WA 99164
www.arch.wsu.edu

Wisconsin

University of Wisconsin-Milwaukee (M.Arch.)
School of Architecture and Urban Planning
P.O. Box 413
Milwaukee, WI 53201
www.uwm.edu/SARUP

CANADA (CACB-ACCREDITED DEGREES)

Carleton University (B.Arch.)
School of Architecture
1125 Colonel By Dr.
Ottawa, ON K1S 6B6
carleton.ca

Dalhousie University (M.Arch.)
DalTech, Faculty of Architecture
P.O. Box 1000
Halifax, NS B3J 2X4
http://architectureandplanning.dal.ca/index.shtml

McGill University (B.Arch.)
School of Architecture
Macdonald-Harrington Building
815 Sherbrooke St. W.
Montreal, QC H3A 2K6
www.mcgill.ca/architecture/

École d'Architecture
Faculté d'Amé
Université de Montréal (B.Arch.)
Faculté de L'Aménagement
2940, Chemin de la Côte Sainte-Catherine
Bureau 2076
Montreal, QC H3T 1T2
www.arc.umontreal.ca/

Université Laval (B.Arch.)
École d'Architecture
Faculté d'Architecture et d'Aménagement
1 Côte de la Fabrique
Quebec, QC G1K 7P2
ulaval.ca

University of British Columbia (M.Arch.)
School of Architecture
6333 Memorial Rd.
Vancouver, BC V6T 1Z2
www.sala.ubc.ca

University of Calgary (M.Arch.)
Faculty of Environmental Design
2500 University Dr. NW
Calgary, AB T2N 1N4
ucalgary.ca

University of Manitoba (M.Arch.)
Faculty of Architecture
201 Russell Building
Winnepeg, MB R3T 2N2
umanitoba.ca

University of Toronto (B.Arch., M.Arch.)
School of Architecture and Landscape Architecture
230 College St.
Toronto, ON N2L 3G1
www.ald.utoronto.ca

University of Waterloo (B.Arch.)
School of Architecture
Faculty of Environmental Sciences
Waterloo, ON N2L 3G1
uwaterloo.ca

ACCREDITED PROGRAMS IN LANDSCAPE ARCHITECTURE

The Landscape Architectural Accreditation Board (LAAB) is recognized by the Council for Higher Education Accreditation (CHEA) as the accrediting agency for first professional baccalaureate and master's degree programs in landscape architecture in the United States. LAAB is a member of the Association of Specialized and Professional Accreditors.

The Board of Trustees of the American Society of Landscape Architects (ASLA) recognizes the quality of educational programs leading to first professional degrees in landscape architecture at the bachelor's or master's level accredited by the Canadian Society of Landscape Architects Accreditation Council (CSLAAC). It regards the criteria for accreditation and many of the individual program guidelines to be comparable to those employed by the LAAB of the ASLA. A list of CSLAAC accredited programs follows the LAAB list. LAAB accredits forty-six programs leading to baccalaureate degrees and twenty-nine leading to master's degrees.

UNITED STATES

Alabama

Auburn University (B.L.A.)
School of Architecture
104 Dudley Hall
Auburn, AL 36849
cadc.auburn.edu

Arizona

Arizona State University (B.S.L.A.)
Landscape Architecture Program
School of Architecture and Landscape Architecture
Tempe, AZ 85287
http://design.asu.edu/sala/index.shtml

University of Arizona (M.L.A.)
School of Landscape Architecture
College of Architecture, Planning, and Landscape Architecture
P.O. Box 210075, Room 104
Tucson, AZ 85721
http://architecture.arizona.edu/landscape/

Arkansas

University of Arkansas (B.L.A.)
Department of Landscape Architecture
School of Architecture
230 Memorial Hall
Fayetteville, AR 72701
http://architecture.uark.edu/

California

California Polytechnic State University (B.S.L.A.)
Department of Landscape Architecture
College of Architecture and Environmental Design
San Luis Obispo, CA 93407
arch.calpoly.edu

California State Polytechnic University (B.S.L.A., M.L.A.)
Department of Landscape Architecture
College of Environmental Design
3801 W. Temple Ave.
Pomona, CA 91768
csupomona.edu

University of California at Berkeley (M.L.A.)
Department of Landscape Architecture
College of Environmental Design
202 Wurster Hall
Berkeley, CA 94720
http://laep.ced.berkeley.edu/

University of California at Davis (B.S.L.A.)
Landscape Architecture Program
Department of Environmental Design
College of Agricultural and Environmental Sciences
One Shields Ave.
Davis, CA 95616
lda.ucdavis.edu

Colorado

Colorado State University, B.S.L.A.
Program in Landscape Architecture
Department of Horticulture and Landscape Architecture
College of Agricultural Sciences
Fort Collins, CO 80523
www.colostate.edu/depts/larch

University of Colorado at Denver (M.L.A.)
Landscape Architecture Program
College of Architecture and Planning
Campus Box 126
P.O. Box 173364
Denver, CO 80217
www.cudenver.edu

Connecticut

University of Connecticut (B.S.L.A.)
Landscape Architecture Program
Department of Plant Science
College of Agriculture and Natural Resources
1376 Storrs Rd., U-67
Storrs, CT 06269
www.cag.uconn.edu

Florida

Florida International University (M.L.A.)
Graduate Program in Landscape Architecture
School of Architecture
University Park Campus
Miami, FL 33199
http://fiu.edu/~soa/

University of Florida (B.L.A., M.L.A.)
Department of Landscape Architecture
College of Architecture
331 Architecture Bldg.
Gainesville, FL 32611
www.dcp.ufl.edu/landscape/

Georgia

University of Georgia (B.L.A., M.L.A.)
Program in Landscape Architecture
School of Environmental Design
609 Caldwell Hall
Athens, GA 30602
www.sed.uga.edu/

Idaho

University of Idaho (B.L.A.)
Landscape Architecture Department
College of Art and Architecture
Moscow, ID 83844
www.caa.uidaho.edu/larch/

Illinois

University of Illinois (B.L.A., M.L.A.)
Department of Landscape Architecture
College of Fine and Applied Arts
101 Buell Hall MC 620, 611 Taft Dr.
Champaign, IL 61820
www.landarch.uiuc.edu/

Indiana

Ball State University (B.L.A., M.L.A.)
Department of Landscape Architecture
College of Architecture and Planning
Muncie, IN 47306
bsu.edu/cap

Purdue University (B.S.L.A.)
Landscape Architecture Program
Department of Horticulture and Landscape Architecture
1165 Horticulture Bldg.
West Lafayette, IN 47907
www.hort.purdue.edu/hort/academics/program.shtml

Iowa

Iowa State University (B.L.A.)
Department of Landscape Architecture
College of Design, Room 146
Ames, IA 50011
www.design.iastate.edu/ARCH/

Kansas

Kansas State University (B.L.A., M.L.A.)
Department of Landscape Architecture/Regional and Community Planning
College of Architecture, Planning, and Design
302 Seaton Hall
Manhattan, KS 66506
http://capd.ksu.edu/

Kentucky

University of Kentucky (B.S.L.A.)
Department of Landscape Architecture
N318 Agriculture Science North
Lexington, KY 40546
www.uky.edu/agriculture/la

Louisiana

Louisiana State University (B.L.A., M.L.A.)
School of Landscape Architecture
College of Design Bldg.
Baton Rouge, LA 70803
http://landscape.lsu.edu/

Maryland

Morgan State University (M.L.A.)
Graduate Program in Landscape Architecture
Montebello Complex, Room B107
Baltimore, MD 21251
http://morgan.edu/academics/IAP/landscape_home.html

University of Maryland (B.L.A., M.L.A.)
Landscape Architecture Program
Department of Natural Resource Sciences and Landscape Architecture
2146 Plant Sciences Bldg.
College Park, MD 20742
www.larch.umd.edu

Massachusetts

Harvard University (M.L.A.)
Department of Landscape Architecture
Graduate School of Design
409 Gund Hall, 48 Quincy St.
Cambridge, MA 02138
gsd.harvard.edu

University of Massachusetts (B.S.L.A., M.L.A.)
Department of Landscape Architecture and Regional Planning
Hills North 109
Amherst, MA 01003
www.umass.edu/larp/

Michigan

Michigan State University (B.L.A.)
Landscape Architecture Program
School of Planning, Design, and Construction
101 Urban and Regional Planning & Landscape Architecture Building
East Lansing, MI 48824
www.spdc.msu.edu/la/

University of Michigan (M.L.A.)
Landscape Architecture
School of Natural Resources and Environment
Dana Bldg., 430 E. University
Ann Arbor, MI 48109
snre.umich.edu/degree_programs/landscape_architecture_3yr/overview

Minnesota

University of Minnesota (M.L.A.)
Department of Landscape Architecture
1425 University Ave. SE, Room 115
Minneapolis, MN 55414
landarch.cdes.umn.edu

Mississippi

Mississippi State University (B.L.A.)
Department of Landscape Architecture
College of Agriculture and Life Sciences
Box 9725
Mississippi State, MS 39762
www.lalc.msstate.edu/

Nevada

University of Nevada, Las Vegas (B.L.A.)
School of Architecture, Sogg Architecture Bldg.
4505 Maryland Pkwy.
Las Vegas, NV 89154
http://architecture.unlv.edu/Site-02/

New Jersey

Rutgers—The State University of New Jersey (B.S.)
Department of Landscape Architecture
Blake Hall, Cook College
93 Lipman Dr.
New Brunswick, NJ 08901
http://landarch.rutgers.edu/

New York

City College of New York (B.S.L.A.)
Urban Landscape Architecture Program
School of Architecture, Urban Design, and Landscape Architecture
138th St. and Convent Ave.
New York, NY 10031
www1.ccny.cuny.edu/prospective/architecture/

Cornell University (B.S.L.A., M.L.A.)
Landscape Architecture Department
440 Kennedy Hall
Ithaca, NY 14853
landscape.cornell.edu

State University of New York (B.L.A., M.L.A.)
Faculty of Landscape Architecture
College of Environmental Science and Forestry
1 Forestry Dr.
Syracuse, NY 13210
fla.esf.edu

North Carolina

North Carolina A & T State University (B.S.L.A.)
Landscape Architecture Program
231 Carver Hall
Greensboro, NC 27411
www.ag.ncat.edu/academics/natres/landarch/index.html

North Carolina State University (B.L.A., M.L.A.)
Landscape Architecture Department, School of Design
P.O. Box 7701
Raleigh, NC 27695
http://ncsudesign.org/content/index.cfm/fuseaction/page/filename/landscape_architecture.html

North Dakota

North Dakota State University (B.L.A.)
Department of Architecture and Landscape Architecture
P.O. Box 5285 S.U. Station
Fargo, ND 58105
http://ala.ndsu.edu/

Ohio

Ohio State University (B.S.L.A., M.L.A.)
School of Landscape Architecture
Austin E. Knowlton School of Architecture
109 Brown Hall, 190 W. Seventeenth Ave.
Columbus, OH 43210
http://knowlton.osu.edu/default.asp?content=18

Oklahoma

Oklahoma State University (B.L.A.)
Landscape Architecture Program, 360 AGH
Stillwater, OK 74078
www.hortla.okstate.edu/

University of Oklahoma (M.L.A.)
Landscape Architecture Program
Gould Hall, Room 162
Norman, OK 73019
http://la.coa.ou.edu/

Oregon

University of Oregon (B.L.A.)
Department of Landscape Architecture
School of Architecture and Allied Arts
Eugene, OR 97403
http://landarch.uoregon.edu/

Pennsylvania

Pennsylvania State University (B.L.A.)
Department of Landscape Architecture
College of Arts and Architecture
210 Engineering Unit D
University Park, PA 16802
www.arch.psu.edu

Temple University (B.S.L.A.)
Department of Landscape Architecture and Horticulture
580 Meetinghouse Rd.
Ambler, PA 19002
www.temple.edu/ambler/la-hort/

University of Pennsylvania (M.L.A.)
Department of Landscape Architecture and Regional Planning
Graduate School of Fine Arts
119 Myerson Hall, 210 S. Thirty-Fourth St.
Philadelphia, PA 19104-6311
www.design.upenn.edu/new/larp/index.php

Rhode Island

Rhode Island School of Design (B.L.A., M.L.A.)
Department of Landscape Architecture
Division of Architecture and Design
2 College St.
Providence, RI 02903
www.risd.edu

University of Rhode Island (B.L.A.)
Landscape Architecture Program
6 Greenhouse Rd., Room 207
Kingston, RI 02881
uri.edu/cels/lar

South Carolina

Clemson University (B.L.A.)
College of Architecture, Arts, and Humanities
Department of Planning and Landscape Architecture
121 Lee Hall, P.O. Box 340511
Clemson, SC 29634
clemson.edu/caah/pla

Texas

Texas A & M University (B.L.A., M.L.A.)
Department of Landscape Architecture and Urban Planning
College of Architecture
311 Langford Architecture Center
College Station, TX 77843
http://archone.tamu.edu/laup/

Texas Tech University (B.L.A.)
Department of Landscape Architecture
College of Agricultural Sciences and Natural Resources
Box 42121
Lubbock, TX 79409
www.larc.ttu.edu

University of Texas—Arlington (M.L.A.)
P.O. Box 19108
Arlington, TX 76019
www.uta.edu/architecture/

Utah

Utah State University (B.L.A., M.L.A.)
Department of Landscape Architecture and Environmental Planning
College of Humanities, Arts, and Social Sciences
Logan, UT 84322
www.usu.edu/laep

Virginia

University of Virginia (M.L.A.)
Department of Landscape Architecture
School of Architecture, Campbell Hall
Charlottesville, VA 22903
www.arch.virginia.edu/landscape/

Virginia Polytechnic Institute and State University (B.L.A., M.L.A.)
Landscape Architecture Department
College of Architecture and Urban Studies
202 Architecture Annex
Blacksburg, VA 24061
www.lar.arch.vt.edu/

Washington

University of Washington (B.L.A., M.L.A.)
Department of Landscape Architecture
College of Architecture and Urban Planning
348 Gould Hall, Box 355734
Seattle, WA 98195
www.caup.washington.edu/larch/

Washington State University (B.L.A.)
Department of Horticulture and Landscape Architecture
College of Agriculture and Home Economics
Johnson Hall 149
Pullman, WA 99164
www.hortla.wsu.edu/

West Virginia

West Virginia University (B.S.L.A.)
Chair of the Landscape Architecture Program
College of Agriculture and Forestry
1142 Agricultural Sciences Bldg.
Morgantown, WV 26506
www.caf.wvu.edu/resm/la/index.html

Wisconsin

University of Wisconsin (B.S.L.A.)
Department of Landscape Architecture
School of Natural Resources
College of Agricultural and Life Sciences
Room 1, Agriculture Hall
1450 Linden Dr.
Madison, WI 53706
www.la.wisc.edu/

CANADA

The following programs are accredited by the Canadian Society of Landscape Architects Accreditation Council (CSLAAC):

Université de Montréal
BLA Program
École d'archtecture de paysage
5620 Ave. Darlington, #3019
C.P. 6128, Succursale A
Montréal, QC H3C 3J7
apa.umontreal.ca

University of British Columbia (M.L.A.)
Landscape Architecture Program
6368 Stores Rd.
Vancouver, BC V6T 1Z4
ubc.ca

University of Guelph (B.L.A., M.L.A.)
School of Landscape Architecture
University of Guelph
Guelph, ON N1G 2W1
uoguelph.ca/landscape_architecture

University of Manitoba (M.L.A.)
Department of Landscape Architecture
Room 220, Architecture II
Winnipeg, MB R3T 2N2
umanitoba.ca

University of Toronto (B.L.A. currently being phased out, M.L.A under review)
Programme in Landscape Architecture
Faculty of Architecture, Landscape, and Design
230 College St.
Toronto, ON M5T 1R2
clr.utoronto.ca